ENDORSE...

"More than a fascinating tutoria... ... scious, Kelly L. Stone's *Thinking* ... ... person needs for finding answers to difficult pro...... offers anyone a way to mine creative information hidden inside the mind. She proves the subconscious can be tapped for brainstorming answers to creative problems."

Dianna Love, *New York Times* bestselling author of *Phantom in the Night* and *Break into Fiction: 11 Steps to Building a Story That Sells*

"Practical, thought-provoking, and easy to use, Kelly L. Stone's *Thinking Write* gives any writer the tools they need to unleash their creativity. If you want to write but have been feeling blocked, this is the book for you!"

CJ Lyons, national bestselling author of *Warning Signs*

"Kelly L. Stone has written a lively owner's manual for the aspiring writer's mind. *Thinking Write* teaches writers how to use the best free tool they've got—not the pen, but the mind. *Thinking Write* shows you how to master your mind."

Stephanie Losee, freelance writer and author of *Office Mate: The Employee Handbook for Finding—and Managing—Romance on the Job*

"Kelly L. Stone has tapped into the deep well of creative wisdom in her new book, *Thinking Write*. Brimming with gems of inspiration and practical guidance, she brings this mysterious process into the hands of anyone willing to follow her thoughtful, clear, and wise counsel. I highly recommend this book for all who seek to improve not only their writing, but the quality of their life."

Dr. Michael Brant DeMaria, psychologist, award-winning composer, author, and speaker

the secret
to
freeing
your
creative

mind

Thinking Write

Kelly L. Stone

Avon, Massachusetts

Published by
Adams Media, a division of F+W Media, Inc.
57 Littlefield Street, Avon, MA 02322. U.S.A.
www.adamsmedia.com

ISBN 10: 1-60550-132-8
ISBN 13: 978-1-60550-132-1

Printed in the United States of America.

J I H G F E D C B A

Library of Congress Cataloging-in-Publication Data
is available from the publisher.

This publication is designed to provide accurate and authoritative information
with regard to the subject matter covered. It is sold with the understanding that
the publisher is not engaged in rendering legal, accounting, or other professional
advice. If legal advice or other expert assistance is required, the services of a com-
petent professional person should be sought.
—From a *Declaration of Principles* jointly adopted by a Committee of the
American Bar Association and a Committee of Publishers and Associations

Many of the designations used by manufacturers and sellers to distinguish their
product are claimed as trademarks. Where those designations appear in this book
and Adams Media was aware of a trademark claim, the designations have been
printed with initial capital letters.

Bird cage © iStockphoto/sonicken
Typewriter © iStockphoto/maystra
Brain © Jupiterimages Corporation

This book is available at quantity discounts for bulk purchases.

For information, please call 1-800-289-0963.

Acknowledgments

I would like to thank my wonderful editors, Katrina Schroeder and Katie Corcoran Lytle, as well as everyone at Adams Media, for acquiring this book and for their continued support of my work; a huge thank you to all of the authors quoted, for taking the time out of their busy schedules to share their thoughts and advice on creativity with me; a warm and heartfelt thanks to Dr. Raymond Moody for allowing me to use his Theater of the Mind research institute as part of my research, and whose work on the link between the subconscious mind and creativity was a great help to me while writing this book; and a very special thank you to Robert M. Stone, MS, for generously sharing with me his extensive knowledge of the mind that helped lay the foundation for many of the techniques presented in this book, for reading early versions of the manuscript and offering suggestions for improvement and accuracy, and for making valuable contributions to many of the chapters as well as the accompanying compact disc.

Contents

The Secret to Freeing Your Creative Mind . . . ix

part i

Your Incredible Mind

CHAPTER ONE: *A Model of Your Mind* . . . 3

CHAPTER TWO: *The Anti-Writer* . . . 14

CHAPTER THREE: *Creativity Is Within Your Grasp* . . . 23

CHAPTER FOUR: *Relaxation: The Foundation for Creativity* . . . 33

part ii

Accessing Your Subconscious Mind

CHAPTER FIVE: *Dream Your Way to Creativity* . . . 47

CHAPTER SIX: *The Creative Pre-sleep State* . . . 62

CHAPTER SEVEN: *Seeing Your Subconscious Mind's Images* . . . 71

CHAPTER EIGHT: *An Easy Subconscious Communication Technique* . . . 81

CHAPTER NINE: *How Nature Inspires Creativity* . . . 91

CHAPTER TEN: *Using Music for Creativity* . . . 101

CHAPTER ELEVEN: *Interacting with Your Characters* . . . 113

part iii

Programming Your Subconscious Mind

CHAPTER TWELVE: *Your Personal Writer's Gold Mine* . . . 125

CHAPTER THIRTEEN: *The Power of Suggestion and Belief* . . . 141

CHAPTER FOURTEEN: *Mental Rehearsal* . . . 150

CHAPTER FIFTEEN: *Creating Sacred Writing Space* . . . 163

CHAPTER SIXTEEN: *Writing Routines for Maximum Creativity* . . . 177

CHAPTER SEVENTEEN: *Collaging and Other Art Forms* . . . 189

AFTERWORD: *Your Creative Mind Toolbox* . . . 203

Bibliography . . . 205

Index . . . 206

The Secret to Freeing Your Creative Mind

As an aspiring writer, what is your most valuable tool? What is the one thing that you absolutely positively cannot do without? Your mind! You can write without a computer, you can write without a typewriter; technically you can even write without a pen and a pad of paper. But you cannot write without your mind.

This book is the owner's manual for this important piece of equipment. More specifically, it tells you how to access your subconscious mind's unlimited resources to help you with three important activities: stimulating your innate creativity, writing what you are called to write, and making progress toward your writing aspirations faster than you ever thought possible.

I wrote this book as a companion to *Time to Write*, in which I tell aspiring writers that no matter how busy they are, they can always find time to write. After I finished that book, a lingering question remained in my mind. I realized that most people, including myself, have to accommodate very limited writing periods around very busy lives. Everyone has to write around jobs, caring for children or elderly parents (or both), taking care of important volunteer duties, exercising, shopping for groceries, doing the laundry, and so forth. Even professional writers have limited time to focus on their works in progress because, after publication, writing becomes a full-time job—the previous books must be marketed, there are appearances to be made, conferences to present at, and signings to attend, while continuing to conduct the daily business of living. Everyone is busy, and everyone needs to make the best use of the writing time that they have been able to carve out of their hectic schedules.

I decided to dig deeper into this issue. As a licensed mental health counselor, I wanted to figure out if there was a way to translate my understanding of the mind and how it operates into a program for writers. Was there a way to show writers how to ignite their creativity? Could I help them meet all of their writing goals no matter how busy they were?

The answer to these questions was yes. As a licensed counselor with twenty years of experience helping people of all ages make improvements in their daily lives, I have an understanding of how the mind works that will benefit you and your writing. Once you have this understanding, you will be able to take full advantage of your innate creativity through the power of your subconscious mind.

All of the techniques I am going to teach you are ones I have used to progress in my writing and to advance my own writing career. They are fun, effective, and most importantly, they allow you to maximize even the briefest writing period by tapping into your powerful subconscious mind. Throughout this book, you'll learn:

- Relaxation techniques and how relaxation is the foundation for tapping into your creative potential
- Easy but innovative techniques for communicating with your subconscious mind—like how to use ideomotor responses and subconscious image projection
- How to stimulate your innate creativity by using nature, music, and other tools that already exist around you
- How to program your subconscious mind for creative gain and goal-achieving purposes
- How to use the power of positive programming and suggestion to reach your writing goals and maximize your chances of success as a writer

Along the way, you'll hear how successful authors use tools like writing routines and other techniques to keep their creative output flowing and how you can apply these methods to your own writing life to get similar results. Some of the writers you'll be hearing from include bestselling authors Allison Brennan,

Tess Gerritsen, Jacquelyn Mitchard, Susan Elizabeth Phillips, Cheryl Holt, Dianna Love, Barbara Freethy, Cathy Maxwell, Kerrelyn Sparks, Brenda Novak, Yasmine Galenorn, Monica McCarty, and many others.

But it is not just contemporary writers who have used the techniques that you will learn in this book; Ernest Hemingway, Charles Dickens, and Robert Louis Stevenson also employed some of these strategies for stimulating their creativity and writing their stories. Even famous inventors such as Henry Ford used some of these techniques. In this book, you will learn how these famous people got their creative juices flowing—and how you can do the same!

There is an accompanying compact disc to this book that is designed to help you put some of these tools that you will be reading about into practice. This companion CD which was written and performed by Robert M. Stone, MS, an expert in subconscious mind communication, will help you learn basic relaxation techniques, the process for accessing your subconscious mind and programming it for writing success, the tool of creative visualization to meet your writing goals (e.g., successfully pitching your book to an agent at a conference), and the technique of subconscious image projection that is presented in Chapter 7. For best results, I recommend that you try the CD after reading the corresponding chapter so you will have an understanding of the techniques you will put into practice.

Are you ready to tap into a portion of your mind that is vastly underutilized by writers, one that will allow you to make strides toward your writing dreams faster than ever? When you're done reading this book, you'll have at your fingertips proven ways to ramp up your creative output, access your personal gold mine of ideas, communicate with and program your subconscious mind—your most powerful writing tool—and everything else you need to get your writing career started, boosted, and infused with unlimited creativity! Let's get started.

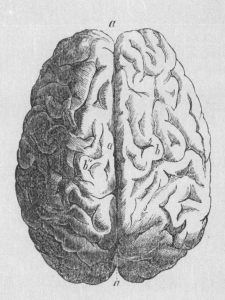

part i

Your Incredible Mind

CHAPTER ONE

A *Model*
of Your
Mind

Your subconscious mind is a powerful ally when it comes to igniting your creativity, and a fertile field of material, ideas, and virtually unlimited resources. However, before you begin learning the techniques that will help you access your subconscious mind, communicate with it, and program it to employ its power, it will be helpful for you to have a basic understanding of the mind: its structure and how it operates.

Contrary to what you may think, understanding how your mind operates is not a daunting task. You do not need to know everything about it for the techniques in this book to work. It's like driving a car. You do not need to understand how the radiator cools the engine, what the spark plugs do, or how the transmission works in order to operate the vehicle. However, you do need to know how to turn on the car, how to steer through traffic, and when to put in gas. Just as you only need this basic information to operate a car, you only need basic information about the mind in order to capitalize on the writing potential that it offers you—the subconscious mind is the vehicle that will take you to success as a writer.

What's on Your Mind?

Have you ever been asked, "What's on your mind?" Most people have. But what exactly is the mind? Sometimes people think that the mind and the brain are the same thing, but there are actually distinct differences between the two. The brain is a physical structure and, because of that, it can be touched, held, and measured. Thanks to modern medicine and high school biology, you probably know what it looks like and maybe even how much it weighs. The brain's various sections have been measured, studied, and labeled according to responsibility: one section controls hearing, a different section is responsible for speech, and so forth.

The mind, however, is not a physical structure. It cannot be seen, held, or weighed. This made it difficult for therapists around the turn of the twentieth century to define the mind and understand how it works so that they could help their clients resolve their problems. At that time, the mind was not well understood. Its functions and responsibilities were not known. No one had studied or measured these functions and responsibilities because it seemed impossible. How can you measure something that you can't see or hold? How could therapists help people get better when they were working with an invisible entity—the mind?

Sigmund Freud, the father of modern psychology, was the first to tackle this dilemma. He decided to give his therapy patients a framework for understanding how their minds worked in order to facilitate the therapy process. Using his background as an experienced analyst, he discovered that there were various portions of the mind that could actually be studied and measured, and that these portions worked in highly specific ways. Freud eventually defined three portions of the mind: the conscious, preconscious, and subconscious, which he called the "unconscious." He cataloged the characteristics of each portion and studied how they operated. By defining how the various portions of the mind worked, Freud was able to help his clients solve their problems by giving them a model that explained the different sections of their minds, what these sections were doing, and why they were doing it.

Perhaps Freud's most significant discovery about the mind was that the portions operate independently from one another and, therefore, can be addressed independently. By working with the sections independently, people could approach problems in a variety of ways, leading to more insight about the problems and creating a more effective and less time-consuming way of resolving them.

From Freud's day to the present, using the various portions of the mind for your personal benefit has endured as a valid and effective approach for bringing about positive change in your life, and it's the key to mastery of your mind for creative purposes. Let's take a closer look at the three parts of the mind that Freud identified.

The Conscious Mind

The conscious mind is the thinking portion of your mind. It is the *me* portion of the mind, with the self awareness of "I think, therefore I am." The primary mechanism of the conscious mind is the field of attention, which is usually directed outward. However, this book will teach you how to direct this attention inward to enhance your effectiveness as a writer.

Basically, the conscious mind is the portion of the mind that you use every day to conduct your life; the conscious field of attention observes the environment, interprets it, and allows you to make decisions. You use your conscious mind when you balance your checkbook, make a grocery list, catch the right commuter train, focus on a business meeting, and watch television with your family at night. Things that pass through your conscious mind's field of attention are easy to recall; for example, you can probably remember what you had for breakfast this morning or what your child wore to school.

The problem is that your field of attention is limited. You can only focus on one thing at a time and your conscious mind can only attend to one thought at a time. Because of this, you are limited in how much information is available to you using only your conscious mind. For example, let's say you are trying to talk on the phone and watch a television show at the same time. If the show is interesting, you hear the person talking on the phone but the content of what they are saying does not register in your conscious mind. You find yourself saying, "what?" a great deal. This is because what your phone caller is saying slips by your field of attention when your attention is focused on the show; you physically hear what is said, but it bypasses your attention. Since your conscious mind can only attend to one thought at a time, at that moment it's whatever is happening on the television.

The opposite is also true. When you're focused on your phone call, the dialogue on the show is not captured by your conscious attention. Your attention shifts back and forth between the TV and your phone call, so at the end of the call, you will remember only a mixture of the show's dialogue and your phone conversation, not the totality of both.

The Preconscious

The preconscious is a layer between the conscious mind and subconscious thought. The preconscious operates independently, meaning that it thinks. This is a very concrete, "all or nothing" part of the mind. Due to this characteristic, it often causes conflict and attempts to interfere with the goals of the conscious mind. This is a very important issue for the writer. I call this interference the "anti-writer" and will discuss it in detail in the next chapter.

In addition to having its own thought processes, all of the things that pass through your conscious field of attention are temporarily stored in the preconscious. This memory storage function is like a storage room of a given size. Items stored here are easy to recall on a short-term basis. Because the capacity of the storage space is finite, the preconscious operates on a "first in, first out" basis.

For example, imagine that your preconscious storage room has ten empty boxes in it. These boxes are of a given size and the information that arrives through the conscious mind is stacked in each box until it is filled to capacity. When box one is filled up with information that has passed through your conscious attention, box two is placed in front of box one, pushing it back a space. As soon as box two gets filled up, it's pushed back by box three, which in turn moves the first box back another space.

This process continues until box ten is filled. When box eleven pushes the line back, box one is pushed completely out of the room and into the subconscious mind's storage space, which is unlimited. The newest information in the preconscious is always closest to consciousness.

The faster the preconscious room fills up, the harder it is to quickly recall the content of the boxes because of the "first in, first out" principle. If all ten boxes fill up quickly, it can be difficult to remember what was stored in box one if it is pushed too far into the subconscious. Say you are cramming for an exam. If you focus on information that is not related to the exam, the preconscious storage area fills up with irrelevant information and the information you need to pass the exam is pushed out of the easy-recall section of the mind.

Information stored in the preconscious mind has always passed through your conscious field of attention. However, because you are bombarded with so much stimuli on a daily basis, much of what you are exposed to is outside of your field of attention and bypasses the preconscious altogether. This information is filed directly into the next component of your mind—the vast subconscious.

The Subconscious Mind

The final component of Freud's mind model is the subconscious. For the writer, this portion of the mind is most important. The subconscious mind is like a giant computer system with multiple input sources. It is constantly recording all of the details of your life, both items that pass through your conscious field of attention and those items that your conscious mind misses entirely. Some items are not subject to easy recall because they have not passed through the conscious field of attention; however, they can be remembered using the specific techniques that you will learn in this book.

The power of the subconscious mind is truly amazing. It monitors and stores everything that goes on around and inside of you. This information is permanent, it is never forgotten, and this is what makes the subconscious mind such a powerful ally to writers.

Let's say that as you're reading this book, there is a storm going on outside. You are focusing your attention on the material in this book. However, while your conscious field of attention is taking in the words on the page and storing them in the preconscious, your subconscious mind is recording the swoosh of the wind, the sound of rain tapping against the glass, the temperature of the room, and hundreds of other nuances that escape your conscious field of attention. Remember, the conscious mind can only attend to one thing at a time and that one thing is reading this book. Only if something draws your attention away from the book—a clap of thunder for instance—will details of the storm pass through your field of attention, get stored in the preconscious, and be subject to easy recall. As soon as you return your attention to the book, the details of the storm again move outside your field of attention, bypass the preconscious, and get stored directly in the subconscious.

The subconscious mind even functions during periods when the conscious mind is asleep or altered in some way. This occurs because the subconscious mind has two major functions: it stores information and it runs your autonomic nervous system, which is responsible for breathing, heart rate, temperature control, and so forth. Since all these functions still have to occur even while you are asleep, your subconscious has to be "on" around the clock; when the conscious mind shuts down through the mechanism of sleep, the subconscious takes over. For example, if your room gets too hot while you're asleep, your body automatically starts to sweat even if you don't wake up. This is your subconscious mind working to control your body temperature. While running your automatic body functions, your subconscious also stores everything else; it records not only the information related to keeping your body alive while you sleep but also all other events going on around you.

What this means for you as a writer, is that your brain is storing material you can use in your work that you may not even realize is there until you look for it. For instance, you suddenly awaken from a deep sleep and find your toddler standing by the bed silently staring at you. The subconscious mind, with its powers of continual observation, alerted your conscious mind that your child needed you and woke you up.

It has also been demonstrated that the subconscious mind functions even when the conscious mind is rendered unconscious during operations. There are documented cases of people under anesthesia who, upon regaining consciousness, reported back with accuracy what was said in the operating room.

A final and valuable characteristic for the writer, is your ability to program your subconscious. The subconscious stores everything and will work to make a reality of whatever you strongly program into it. Many people have documented this powerful feature of the subconscious mind, and have developed techniques to benefit from it. Motivational speakers and authors throughout history have discussed this critical foundational concept: whatever you think about continually becomes your reality. You would program your subconscious mind to create a reality that consists of you finding success as a writer. I will cover this concept in more depth in Chapters 12 and 13.

Accessing Your Subconscious Is Key to Creativity

Automatic subconscious storage of most of the details of life is a survival skill that allows humans to function effectively. It is simply impossible for your conscious mind to register all of the information that bombards you on a daily basis. If you consciously paid attention to every single thing that went on around you at all times, you couldn't focus on any given task or get anything done. To function, the conscious mind selects what is most important and the subconscious mind takes care of the rest.

However—and this is why learning to access your subconscious mind is the key to your unlimited creativity—all of the information that you are exposed to on a day-to-day basis is stored and accessible to you via your subconscious. All of this information can be retrieved with the techniques presented in this book, which opens up your own private treasure trove of rich creative material. Whatever genre you write in, using subconscious recall can help you as an aspiring author. All writers write about what they know to a great extent. Tapping into subconscious memories and recorded events brings richness to characters and stories that is simply not possible when the conscious recall mechanism is used alone.

How can accessing your subconscious mind's stored details enrich your creative writing endeavors? Let's say you want to write a personal essay about an event from your past—your sister's wedding that occurred ten years ago. If you remember the event using only your conscious mind, you will recall some of the main details that passed through your field of attention, such as the color of the dresses, perhaps who caught the bouquet, what the wedding cake looked like, and so forth. But many of the sharper and richer details, the kind that would enhance your storytelling, escape your conscious recall.

The Voice of Experience

"My subconscious does a lot of my plotting for me."

—Yasmine Galenorn, *USA Today* bestselling author of *Night Huntress* and other novels

If you tap into your subconscious mind using the techniques that you will learn in this book and look at the same event, you will be able to remember everything about the wedding because everything was recorded and filed away into the subconscious. Your memory, and in turn your writing, will be greatly enhanced by details that you can pull up from your subconscious.

By accessing the memory of the wedding through your subconscious mind, you can recall the smell of the flowers, the color patterns of the sunlight through the stained glass windows, the temperature of the air in the church, the details of the guests in the pews, how your shoes pinched your feet, background noises such as a baby crying, the minister's tone of voice as he recited the ceremony, the sound of your mother crying softly into her handkerchief, the sputtering sound the candles made, the feel of the breeze off the lake at the reception, the woodsy taste of the wine, and so forth. All of the things that your conscious mind missed during the actual event and the items that escaped your field of attention because you were focused on the main activities can be remembered because all of these details are stored by the subconscious mind. Your subconscious recorded every aspect of the wedding and retrieving this detailed information will allow you to recreate the event in words.

It's this recording of every detail that brings a wealth of information to the creative process. Tapping into the total picture of a scene lets you build that scene with words that bring it alive. As the adage says, a picture is worth a thousand words. As a writer, you have to build the picture with words, and accessing your subconscious mind gives you all the words you need to paint vivid pictures of your own.

Your most valuable tool as a writer is your subconscious mind. It is the eternal fountain of creativity. Its memory banks store the words you need to create literary masterpieces, and it's a dynamic force that will help you reach all of your writing goals.

Now that you have a basic understanding of how the mind works, let's move on to the last component of the mind: your anti-writer.

The Writer's Block

As a writer, your subconscious mind is your most valuable tool. Learning to tap into this vast resource of creative material is like tapping into your own personal gold mine of ideas, inspiration, and creativity. To use your subconscious for maximum creativity, you need a basic understanding of how the mind operates. Remember:

- Sigmund Freud created a model of the mind that included the conscious, the preconscious, and the subconscious.

- The subconscious mind records everything going on around you at all times; learning to access this material can enrich your writing and inspire your creativity.

- The subconscious mind is invaluable to a writer because, among other things, it can be programmed to help you reach your writing goals.

CHAPTER TWO

The *Anti-Writer*

Are your writing sessions not as productive as you would like them to be? Do you doubt your ability to become a successful writer? Do you ever think there is nothing left to write about? If so, you are under the influence of your anti-writer.

The anti-writer originates in the preconscious and is the portion of your mind that opposes you, working to create doubt, fear, and failure. This part of everyone's mind holds negative ideas and beliefs that affect his or her self-concept. Some psychologists have called this the dark side or the shadow side of human nature. For our purposes, this is the part of your mind that holds you back or that does things that subtly undermine your attempts to become a writer.

Keeping your anti-writer under control is an important key to accomplishing your writing goals. Everything that passes from your subconscious into your conscious mind must pass through the preconscious. If this anti-writer portion is not controlled or minimized, it can interfere with using your subconscious mind for maximum creative gain. Fortunately, it is not necessary to know all the whys and wherefores of the anti-writer in order to reduce its impact. You only need to recognize its interference and take action to reduce its effect on your writing.

Can't Never Could

A clear indicator of the anti-writer at work is doubt. If you think you can't do something or aren't good enough to be successful, these feelings are coming from your anti-writer.

As you know, the subconscious mind is a powerful source of creativity for writers, and the anti-writer attempts to block access to this wonderful resource. It sneakily does this by trying to make you think that others can do things that you can't. If you fall for this line from the anti-writer, you won't make the effort needed to access your subconscious mind and you won't benefit from its creative power. If you allow your anti-writer to convince you that the techniques discussed in this book won't work for you, they won't.

The Voice of Experience

"I always hit some point where I know the book is awful and cannot be saved. I ignore this. I keep writing."

—Lori Devoti, romance and fantasy author of *Wild Hunt* and other novels

Here are some other ways that the anti-writer portion of your mind interferes with your efforts to become a successful writer:

- *Resistance to writing.* You have scheduled an hour to write but at the appointed time slot, you suddenly decide that you must do the laundry immediately.
- *Sneakily sabotaging your writing efforts.* You were making a sandwich before you sat down to write and "accidentally" knocked the jar of mustard off the counter, ensuring that the kitchen floor would have to be mopped right this instant. The upset and aggravation wrecks your creative flow.
- *Setting yourself up for failure before you try.* This is the result of constant negative thoughts; you have already tried something and it didn't work, so why bother doing it again? For example, you may try the exercises on the CD, but by not allowing yourself to get into the flow of it, you prevent any progress you could make to access your subconscious creativity.

The anti-writer portion of your mind can be a very powerful force if you do not control it. The negative statements that it makes can actually program your subconscious mind, which then works to bring the negative statements into reality. If you repeatedly tell yourself that there's no point in trying to learn to be more creative, that nothing will help you to access your subconscious mind, or that, unlike you, everybody who has ever been published is simply lucky so why bother, then your subconscious mind will work to create that situation for you. It accepts the anti-writer statements just as it does the positive statements that you will learn in Chapter 13.

Counteracting Your Anti-Writer

The key to not allowing the anti-writer to sabotage your efforts and progress is to recognize it and take an active stance against it. You do this by bringing all of the negative statements you tell yourself about your writing into your awareness. Remember, there is no such thing as a small negative statement. They add up and can be very destructive to your writing career. Let's discuss some ways to identify and combat these anti-writer statements.

Keep an Anti-Writer Notebook

The first thing you need to do is to identify all the different ways that your anti-writer makes itself known. Purchase a small spiral notebook that can fit into your purse or briefcase and keep it with you at all times. Every day for two weeks, write down all the negative thoughts and comments that you make to yourself about your writing or your abilities as a writer—no matter how small or inconsequential you feel they are. This includes any negative statement you make to yourself such as "I will never get my book written," as well as comments that you may make related to other people's writing. For example, you may see a new author on the *New York Times* bestseller list and think: "They must know somebody in the publishing business." These types of comments reinforce myths about how successful writers earned their success. If you follow this train of thought, the only conclusion you can draw is that someone cannot become a successful writer unless he or she has connections in the publishing industry, so *why should you bother*. Do you see how this type of thinking automatically sets you up for failure?

After a few days you will be able to recognize themes and patterns in your own negative self-talk. As you identify and write down your anti-writer statements, the next step is to verbally counter them.

Write Countering Statements on Index Cards

At the end of two weeks, transfer all the negative, sabotaging comments you've made to yourself to a clean sheet of paper.

Draw a line down the center of the paper to make two columns. Label the left side "anti-writer" and the right side "writer." For every negative statement in the anti-writer column, construct a counter or neutralizing statement and put it in the writer column. For example:

Anti-Writer	Writer
Why bother? I'm never going to get published anyway	I love writing and I will be successful as an author
I can never relax	I am learning to be a relaxed, creative person
I just don't have the time to write with my busy schedule	I know there is time in my day to write and I will find it
This essay has been rejected four times already. What's the point in sending it out again?	If I persist, I will eventually find an editor who likes my work.

Looking at the statements in your anti-writer column will give your conscious mind a clear idea of just what your anti-writer is doing to interfere with your writing success. Immediately countering the statement will set up a habit of neutralizing these negative thoughts. Make your own list based on what your anti-writer has been telling you.

To keep actively counteracting the anti-writer statements, transfer the positive, supportive comments to index cards and carry them with you at all times. Pull them out and review them every chance you get: on breaks at work, while waiting on your meal to arrive at lunch, and before you go to bed each night. These positive statements will help counteract the negative comments put forth by your anti-writer.

You can even make use of your drive time by recording your positive writer statements on a digital recorder and repeatedly playing them. Remember, the more positive input you give your subconscious mind, the more it will work to make that positive situation a reality for you.

List Your Sabotaging Actions

During the two weeks you are monitoring your anti-writer statements, you also need to keep a list of all the ways that you sabotage your efforts at writing. The spilled mustard on the kitchen floor is one example. Another is setting your alarm clock to get up an hour early so you can write before work and then hitting the snooze button six times in a row, or worse, turning the alarm off in your sleep. Or maybe you planned to write in the evening after your family was in bed, but your child demands some ice cream and there's none in the house. Instead of letting your spouse handle this request, you charge off to the grocery store and lose your writing time.

Take detailed notes on what you did to sabotage your writing efforts so you can look for patterns. One way that I sometimes sabotage my early morning writing efforts is by staying up too late the night before. Because I have to get up so early in order to have time to write before I leave for work, if I do not get into bed early enough the night before I can't get up the next morning; or if I do get up, I'm so tired that I'm not productive. Do you see how staying up too late would go down on my list of sabotaging activities?

You may be sabotaging your creativity in more subtle ways as well. You may regularly sit down at your desk to write, but lose focus once there. You check e-mail, rearrange the pens on your desk, or get lost on the Internet doing research. Maybe you edit one piece over and over without moving on to anything new, thinking that it has to be perfect before you can send it out. Maybe you write half-heartedly, believing deep down that you will never reach your goals. Maybe you don't push yourself to achieve new heights in your writing by never stretching out of your comfort zone.

If things like this happen every once in a while, it's not a big deal. If in two weeks you list one sabotaging activity and it never comes up again, don't worry about it. You are going to feel off your game occasionally, and part of accessing your creative mind is knowing when to take a break from your project so the well can refill. Problems develop, though, when these types of behaviors become a habit, because they start to negatively impact your writing output and your level of creativity. So pay close attention to the sabotaging activities that you list three or more times in two weeks.

Make an Action Plan

At the end of the two weeks, you will have identified some patterns of sabotaging behavior. Now it is time to generate an action plan. Your plan can consist of anything that helps you combat your anti-writer. It can range from setting an alarm clock to remind you when it's time to start writing, to pulling out your supportive index cards when you are at your desk and repeating the anti-writer countering statements over and over again. On your plan, write down anything that will help you reduce the effects of your anti-writer.

You may be wondering why it's important to write down your anti-writer plan. You want to do this because a written plan is infinitely more powerful than a plan that exists solely in your mind. Just the fact that you took the time to write it down reinforces to your subconscious mind that you are serious about it. If you don't write it down, your anti-writer will sabotage your writing efforts by making you forget your plan. For example, you may decide that you will be at your writing desk by 10 P.M. no matter what, but the first night you want to implement this plan you find it's suddenly 11 P.M. and time for bed. The ten o'clock hour came and went without you noticing. That's the anti-writer at work. It sabotaged your writing efforts by making you lose track of time.

Once your write down your plan, hang it in a place where you will see it frequently. Hanging it up so you won't forget reminds you constantly of your plan. You can make a sign to hang on the wall or write the plan on index cards and review it every night along with your countering statements. All methods of input are helpful to get the positive messages through to your subconscious mind.

For my example of staying up too late, I will write out a plan that involves setting the alarm clock at night to tell me when it's time to get into bed. I will then alert my family that I have to be in bed by a certain time and that all my evening activities must be scheduled to allow me to do that. I hang this plan on the wall by my computer. Then I discipline myself to get into bed when the alarm rings.

Remember that the anti-writer is a portion of your mind that sabotages your writing efforts and stifles your creativity. Becoming consciously aware of its negative statements and sabotaging behavior allows you to make an effective plan to counteract it. Control your anti-writer and you will become a successful writer.

The Writer's Block

The anti-writer is a portion of your mind that originates in the preconscious, working against your efforts to become a writer by creating doubt about your abilities. It's the part of your mind that holds you back or does things that subtly undermine your attempts to become a writer. Keeping your anti-writer under control is an important key to accomplishing your writing goals, and there are easy ways to do this. Remember, it's important to:

- Identify the sabotaging actions your anti-writer takes by listing on index cards the negative statements you make to yourself about your potential as a writer.

- Make an action plan to counter these statements.

- Hang your list somewhere that you will always see it.

CHAPTER THREE

Creativity

Is Within Your

Grasp

O ne of the main roadblocks to creativity is the idea that the time you spend in your creative endeavors is not useful or productive. Aspiring writers often feel guilty for leaving family or social obligations to devote time to their works in progress. Creativity is often relegated to last on your to-do list because you cannot justify the time you spend doing it. So why should you learn how to free your creative mind?

Why Create?

The *Oxford American Dictionary* defines the word "create" as: "to bring into existence, to originate, to produce by what one does." A product that did not exist before is brought as an idea from the misty realm of the mind into physical form, something that you can see, hold, and touch. Nikola Tesla was a noted electrical engineer who mentally constructed the alternating current electrical system using his subconscious mind; he worked out all the details in his subconscious and then built the actual components that worked the first time he tried them. The electricity that is used today is generated by Tesla's system, unchanged since 1895. The Wright Brothers wondered what it would be like to fly and built a working model of the modern-day airplane.

Humans were designed to create. It's what we do. Everything that exists in daily life is a creation: your computer, the painting on your living room wall, the running water in your house, the buttonholes on your coat, your car, your radio, the central air in your office building—all of these things were once just an idea in someone's mind. Not all creations are as concrete as a car or a painting. Writers wonder "what if?" and make up stories that entertain the world. Author Yasmine Galenorn saw a license plate that read "hunter" and created a fictional story around it by wondering "what if?" the owner was a serial killer taunting the police.

As one idea is turned into a creation, more ideas are produced. This happens because the source of your creativity is your subconscious mind. Maximum writing creativity occurs when you learn to tap into your subconscious and access the unlimited supply of ideas and inspiration that *already exist* within you. It's a well that never runs dry. Most successful writers say that they have more ideas than they could ever get to in their entire lives. "I used to believe that I only had so many ideas for books and that eventually I would run out," says Molly O'Keefe, award-winning author of *Worth Fighting For* and other novels. "But creativity, like so many things, gives back when you use it. The more I wrote, the more ideas I had. So now, when I'm done with a project I usually have another idea waiting for me."

As you begin to access and use the power of your subconscious mind, this will happen for you, too.

Written creations such as articles, essays, poems, and books also produce the intangible. They often educate people or facilitate in readers a new understanding about certain concepts. For example, nonfiction writers investigate events or issues and create articles and books that inform and educate people about the subject. Writing as creating is a circular system, too. The creation keeps on creating. It starts with the writer, passes to the reader, and comes full circle back to the writer. This happens because most authors feel that acknowledgment, thanks, and praise from a reader create the deepest contentment and fulfillment in their lives. Writers often say after receiving a complimentary e-mail or comment at a bookstore, "That is the reason I write."

The Voice of Experience

"You have to give yourself time to create."

—Cathy Maxwell, *New York Times* bestselling author of *Bedding the Heiress* and other novels

There are actually dozens of reasons to tune in, cultivate, and nurture the source of your creativity, no matter what your long-term writing goals may be. Most successful authors would keep writing even if they never got published again because the act of creating is its own reward.

Benefits of Creating

Acting on your desire to be creative is fulfilling because it manifests your creativity in a concrete form that is personally rewarding. This is the key benefit to creation of any kind; you have accomplished something. You have brought into existence a book, a poem, a painting, a sculpture, a bookcase. Something that had existed only in your mind now exists in the world, which creates a wonderful feeling of pride and satisfaction.

The Voice of Experience

"Anything can spark creativity. It's always there."

—Yasmine Galenorn

There are emotional benefits to tapping into your subconscious source of creativity on a regular basis. When you touch that creative part of yourself, you feel more complete. By utilizing your subconscious mind, you will make steady progress toward completing your novel, your collection of poems, or your family's memoirs. When you program your subconscious mind to help you write regularly, you will meet your writing goals, whatever they may be. When you meet your writing goals you will feel happier, more content, and fulfilled.

You may also want to create because:

- You need a method of self-expression.
- You want to satisfy your Burning Desire to Write (that feeling that you can't *not* write).
- Bringing an idea to fruition creates a sense of deep satisfaction.
- Writing gives you a tangible product that lasts over time.
- Setting and reaching writing goals adds value and meaning to your life.

Some people seem to know intuitively what they need to be creative; they sense what environmental and internal factors must exist to allow the creative parts of their minds to emerge. Others learn what conditions will trigger their creativity through trial and error, many times as children. However, by the time most people reach adulthood they have forgotten how to access their creative selves, and the daily routine of work, caring for families, paying bills, and doing laundry has helped bury creativity under a mountain of the mundane. But the good news is that accessing your creativity and becoming creative can be relearned. You can set up the conditions that will allow your creative mind to emerge. You can do exercises that will stimulate your creativity. You can program your subconscious mind to help you become more creative. Creativity is within your grasp because it is already within you.

Characteristics of Creative People

Motivation theorists have documented the fact that creative people share some common characteristics. As you read, determine how many of these traits you already notice in your own creative process.

Creative people:

- *Have a wide range of interests.* They are curious about a variety of topics and activities. It's not unusual for writers to also pursue painting, sewing, knitting, beading, and other hobbies that produce a visual, tangible result. Many authors also tackle gardening and baking projects, especially as a way to transition from an intense writing period back into their daily routine.
- *Combine facts and ideas in unique ways.* People who are more in tune with their innate creativity look at the ordinary and leap to the extraordinary. They approach life with a

whimsical, off-center way of looking at things that produces fresh ideas.

- *Have a high tolerance for frustration, chaos, and complexity.* Any
creative project usually starts out as a nebulous, confusing
mess, and creative people in all fields are okay with this.
They can tackle that mess day in and day out until the *ah-
ha* moment strikes.

- *Are patient while waiting for the "eureka moment."* Creative people are patient when determining how to untangle a problem in their work. Their tolerance for the initial chaos that
accompanies any creative period is great. Even though
they may feel uncomfortable with it, they trust their process and believe that eventually it will work itself out if
they just keep at it.

- *Expect to receive hunches and intuitive thoughts.* When faced
with problems in their projects, creative people simply
wait it out. They turn the problem over to their subconscious mind and then pay attention to whatever comes to
them. The hallmark of a creative person is that they *expect*
to receive inspiration and, because they expect it, inspiration arrives. This is a habit that can be learned.

- *Act on hunches and intuitive thoughts even if they don't understand
them.* Creative people learn to listen to and trust their inner
voice. When they get that "gut feeling" they pay attention
and act upon it. Even if they do not understand why or
how, they accept that the creative process knows best and
they follow its lead. Usually the results turn out better than
they expect, too. For example, the late photographer Dorothea Lange trusted a hunch to turn down a deserted road
in California and discovered the now famous migrant family who became a photographic icon of the Depression.

- *Honor and trust their creative process.* Creative people learn
what works and what doesn't by observing their own pro-

cess. They are willing to go along with their creative meandering and give it space in their lives.

- *Are self-starters.* Creative people do not need an external source to motivate them to work on their ideas. They can put wheels on ideas. They get excited about their musings and go to work to bring their ideas to fruition.

Henry Ford, the inventor of the automobile, is a good example of the type of creativity that can come from the characteristics defined above. Ford had an idea for a horseless carriage and, after the first Model T rolled off the lines, he pressed further and came up with a vision of what is now known as the V-8 motor. The idea for this machine worked on paper, but his engineers in the lab found that they could not manufacture the physical representation of the idea. No matter what they tried or how they tried it, they simply could not create the motor that Ford had drawn on paper.

After six months, the engineers approached Ford and told him that it couldn't be done. Ford, who was absolutely determined to produce this motor, told them to keep working on it until they had succeeded. The engineers went back to work and toiled away for another six months. Finally, the "eureka moment" arrived and they found the solution that they needed to produce Ford's vision.

The Voice of Experience

"Staring at the ceiling counts as my meditation, and I do it pretty often, whenever I get into trouble with the story."

—Tess Gerritsen, internationally bestselling author of *The Bone Garden* and other novels

Ford had an intuition that he refused to ignore. He was tolerant and patient with the chaos of the creative process. Most importantly, he trusted and honored his own creative hunches.

Kristen Painter, cofounder of RomanceDivas.com and an author who has been a finalist in multiple writing contests, is an example of how inspiration combined with tenacity can bring success to the writing process. She says, "I don't get stuck. In fact, I don't actually believe in writer's block. I think you can force your way through those tough spots. Yes, you might come to a spot where you don't know what happens, but that can be worked out. You can always write something, and that something can always be edited. It's hard to edit a blank page."

Painter goes on to explain how she works to bring her initial vision to fruition, just like Ford did. "My 'ah-ha' moments tend to come at the very beginning, at the birth stage of the book. My 'ah-has' are more like, 'Wow, that would be a great idea for a book.' Then the story unfolds from there," she says. "There might be 'ah-has' along the way, but they tend to be smaller, something that would connect two scenes as opposed to making the whole story work."

Learning to live with the chaos of creativity, especially in the form of writer's block as Painter does, is one of the hallmarks of a creative person and a successful writer.

When you learn to access and use the power of your subconscious, your creative writing abilities become limitless because your subconscious mind has no limits and no boundaries. You will be able to imagine possibilities and create new realities from those possibilities both in your work and in your steps to writing success.

There are many reasons to devote time to your creative writing endeavors, not the least of which is that you will fulfill your Burning Desire to Write and meet your writing goals. Focusing on your creative capabilities enhances your life by bringing you that wonderful feeling of accomplishment. And much as painters need time to stretch their canvas, collect their paints, clean their brushes, and so forth, writers need creative time to research, reflect on their ideas, flesh out outlines, and edit their previous work. Remember that even during the busiest day, you can still find time to touch your creativity, because the techniques in this book will make even the smallest amount of writing time fruitful and productive and worth your undivided attention.

The Writer's Block

There are many reasons to carve out time to devote to your creative endeavors, most importantly because it generates a sense of accomplishment. Creating through writing fulfills your Burning Desire to Write—that feeling that you can't not write. Also, remember that creative people share some common characteristics. For example:

- They trust their hunches and act on them, even when they do not understand them.

- They expect to receive hunches and trust their intuition.

- They are comfortable with the initial chaos that accompanies any creative task, and are patient while they wait for the "eureka moment" to arrive.

CHAPTER FOUR

Relaxation:
The Foundation for
Creativity

Y ou may be surprised to learn that something as simple as relaxation is the foundation that allows creativity to bubble up. A relaxed body and mind are essential to creating a state of mind conducive to creativity. Learning to relax also lays the foundation for using the other techniques in this book that will allow you to access and program your subconscious mind, and build a bridge to lifelong creativity.

In the hectic world we live in today, most people have forgotten how to really relax. Achieving a truly relaxed state takes concentrated effort and focus. Fortunately, a relaxed mind and body can be easily achieved through the systematic and progressive relaxation of the major muscle groups of your body. Tracks one and two on the accompanying CD are also designed to assist you in learning this process.

Relaxation for Maximum Creativity

You have to relax in order to bypass the conscious and preconscious and access your subconscious mind. Remember, the preconscious—your anti-writer—is looking for ways to keep your conscious mind from your subconscious mind. It is like a malicious gatekeeper. It is the part of your mind that sabotages your best efforts to succeed. Relaxation allows you to bypass the preconscious mechanism and gain direct access to your subconscious mind.

The Voice of Experience

"When I'm relaxed and feeling positive about my abilities, then the creativity flows."

—Kerrelyn Sparks, *New York Times* bestselling author of *The Undead Next Door* and other novels

You have likely spontaneously experienced this phenomenon. Think of a time when you were faced with a difficult problem that really stumped you. You may have tried to come up with a solution to the problem for weeks to no avail, and then the solution came to you suddenly while you were in the shower, indulging in a long hot soak, exercising, or when you were doing something fun like skateboarding with your kid. During times like this, the body relaxes, which allows your brain to shift into a state of mind that is conducive to creativity. Solutions that were once elusive will literally pop into your conscious mind.

Some people refer to this as the left-brain/right-brain phenomenon. The left side of your brain is believed to be responsible for logical, linear thought and not associated with creativity, whereas the right side of the brain is believed to think in more abstract terms and is therefore capable of making creative leaps that the left brain cannot. Physically relaxing the body allows you to stimulate right-brain thinking and go directly to the source of your creativity—your subconscious mind. Using the methods in this book, you will learn how to have these right-brain experiences at will.

Brain Waves and Creativity

Even though the mind and the brain are two separate entities, the mind manifests itself through the brain and therefore gives you a concrete mechanism to work with in terms of stimulating your creativity. The brain gives off electricity that is measured by an electroencephalography, or EEG, machine in waves according to frequency. Certain frequencies are associated with creativity and are found only when the body is relaxed.

The four types of brain waves are:

- *Delta waves.* These brain waves indicate a fully alert, conscious person. The body is ready for action. You would exhibit these types of brain waves in a job interview, at a meeting with your child's teacher, or when you're about to give a presentation to a group of people. Delta waves indicate left-brain activity and do not produce spontaneous creativity.
- *Alpha waves.* These brain waves indicate that you are alert but your body is more relaxed. For example, you might be sitting on the beach watching the sunset or taking a stress-relieving stroll through a park after a tense meeting at work. Alpha waves are associated with creativity and right-brain activity.

- *Theta waves.* These brain waves typically indicate deep sleep where the body is fully relaxed but the brain is engaged, such as rapid-eye-movement (REM) sleep where dreaming occurs. Theta waves have also been found in people who are meditating or doing activities that require concentrating on one task for a long period of time. They could account for the reason many people have bursts of insight when driving on the interstate.
- *Beta waves.* These waves indicate deep, nondreaming sleep and are not associated with creativity.

Many people have learned how to use relaxation of the body to produce alpha and even theta brain waves, thereby increasing focus and concentration and stimulating creativity. For instance, people who learn to fire walk often exhibit alpha brain waves while walking across the hot coals. Experienced meditators have learned to use relaxation to perform extraordinary physical feats, such as being buried alive without oxygen for up to twelve hours at a time with no harm. Elite athletes have been documented to have a burst of alpha wave activity in the seconds before they perform a feat requiring high amounts of skill, such as throwing a basketball through the hoop or taking a difficult putt.

This isn't just true for athletes. It's true for you too. Think back to a time when you felt stressed to produce a solution to a problem that your company was facing. Maybe the stress arose during a tense meeting late on Friday when an unexpected issue occurred that had to be resolved by close of business that day. It's difficult to be creative under pressured conditions like that. You may think of something to provide a temporary solution, but chances are it's not as good as what you'll come up with over the weekend, when you have a chance to rest, relax, and allow your subconscious mind to work on the problem.

This is the basis for the concept of "sleeping on" a problem. While your subconscious mind can always come up with the answer to a problem or a find a unique way of solving an issue, when you're stressed out, your brain is in a state and focused outward on the environment. There can be no flow or exchange of ideas between your conscious and subconscious minds. After you sleep for a while and your brain waves slow down, then your subconscious mind can easily communicate with your conscious mind.

Progressive Relaxation

Because it's not always easy to dash off and take a nap, learning progressive relaxation can come in handy. Once you learn how to do it, you can adapt it to your own individual needs. For instance, if you have scheduled a block of time to write and be creative and there is no time pressure on you, you can use the full progressive relaxation program on track two of the CD to get into a deeply relaxed state before you create. Track two is the full-length program and shows you how to use a full progressive relaxation system. If you only have thirty minutes to write, you can do a quick relaxation like the one on track one to focus your attention on the work at hand for maximum use of those thirty minutes. This track is a short and simple relaxation technique that helps you recognize and induce a relaxed state of mind. In the beginning, when you are starting to learn and use this process, use the long program on the CD (track two), which should take about twenty-five minutes. Because these techniques may be new to you, the instructions are presented in written form below, but after you become adept at using the procedure, you can work on your own and decrease the amount of time that it takes for you to get into a relaxed state.

When using progressive relaxation prior to starting a writing session, ensure that you have set up the following conditions:

- *Eliminate intrusions.* Unplug your phone, turn off your cell phone, and ask family members not to disturb you during this time. Go to a private room in the house that has a comfortable bed or chair that you can recline in for the relaxation period. Your own bed is fine as long as you can stay awake. You may want to prop the pillows up behind your back so that you are in a semi-sitting position.
- *Get comfortable.* You want to support your head and neck by leaning back on a pillow or headrest. Crossing your limbs or folding your feet under you will cut off your circulation and cause you to have to move, so leave your arms by your side or fold your hands in your lap, and let your feet and legs rest uncrossed in a position that feels natural to you.
- *Ensure adequate time.* If you have to go somewhere in an hour, it will be difficult to relax since that time commitment will be pressing on you. Arrange to learn progressive relaxation during a time of day when you can let go and indulge yourself in the process.
- *Use the restroom before you begin.*

Once you are comfortable and have set up your environment to ensure zero distractions, you are ready to begin the process.

Full Program

Following are the instructions for total progressive relaxation. Once you read through them, pop in the enclosed CD and practice. It may take you several times to learn to do this. The mind tends to wander, so you must exercise discipline to stay focused on relaxing. You may also notice tensions in your body that you were unaware of previously. This is a normal occurrence. If you need to move or shift positions during the relaxation, do so mindfully and quickly.

1. Begin by focusing your attention on your breathing. Do not try to control it, just watch the natural in-and-out flow. Begin saying to yourself, "I'm beginning to relax now. I'm beginning to relax now."

2. Mentally ask your subconscious mind to begin relaxing your feet. Say something like, "Subconscious, begin relaxing my feet. Allow all of the muscles of my feet and toes to loosen and relax." Focus your attention on your feet and feel them begin to loosen and relax. Continue to mentally repeat, "I'm beginning to relax now. I'm beginning to relax now."

3. Next ask your subconscious mind to relax your legs. Say, "Subconscious, relax my legs. Allow all of the muscles of my calves and thighs to loosen and relax." Feel the tension in your lower limbs ease. Continue to mentally repeat, "I'm beginning to relax now. I'm beginning to relax now."

4. Now ask your subconscious mind to relax your lower back muscles. Allow the muscles of your lower back to loosen and relax. Continue to mentally repeat, "I'm beginning to relax now. I'm beginning to relax now."

5. Now ask your subconscious mind to relax your upper back and shoulder muscles. Allow all the muscles of your upper back and shoulders to loosen and relax. Continue to mentally repeat, "I'm beginning to relax now. I'm beginning to relax now."

6. Continue in this fashion by relaxing your stomach muscles next, then your chest and breathing muscles, then your arms and hands, then your neck, and last your head and facial muscles. After each body segment, repeat, "I'm beginning to relax now. I'm beginning to relax now."

7. When you have finished working your way through your body, shift your focus back to your breathing and repeat ten times, "Relaxing more and more and going to a deeper and deeper level. Relaxing more and more and going to a deeper and deeper level."

8. Take three slow, deep breaths. You should now be in a state of relaxed focus. Stay in this state of relaxation for at least fifteen minutes (you can set an alarm clock if necessary.) Just enjoy the relaxation. If you feel yourself drifting off to sleep, straighten your spine and bring your awareness back to your breathing. Focus your attention wherever your breathing is most noticeable to you; it could be the in-and-out sensation of air in your nose, the rise and fall of your chest, or the up and down movement of your stomach. Simply focus your awareness on the breath and allow yourself to sink into deep relaxation.

9. When you have completed at least fifteen minutes in a relaxed, focused state, bring yourself back to a normal state of awareness by counting backward from ten. When you reach one, open your eyes, and retain the positive feelings that come with being relaxed. You are now ready to focus on your writing for the day.

Short Progressive Relaxation

You can use a short version of progressive relaxation whenever you have limited time to write and need to get into a creative mind state quickly, when you are writing in public and need to get into hyper-focus on the manuscript before you, when you take a break from writing and need to refresh your brain, or any time you want to access your subconscious mind for help with writing-related tasks.

To do the short version, find a comfortable chair or make yourself comfortable wherever you are sitting. Close your eyes. If that's not possible because of the environment, lower your eyelids and stare at a spot on the floor. Put your feet on the floor and let your hands rest in your lap. Soften your gaze. Draw your attention to your breathing. Focus your awareness on the area of your body where your breathing is most noticeable; it might be your chest, your stomach, or your nose. Let your mind go and keep your attention on your breathing. Mentally repeat, "I'm beginning to relax now. I'm beginning to relax now."

After a few minutes, begin asking your subconscious to relax your feet, legs, lower back, upper back, stomach, chest and breathing muscles, and so forth until you have completed your entire body. Depending on the environment and how much time you have, this can take as long as you need it to or it can be done quickly by mentally touching on each muscle group.

When you complete the body relaxation, repeat to yourself several times, "Relaxing more and more and going to a deeper and deeper level." This statement should trigger your brain into an alpha frequency state, the state conducive to creativity. When you feel relaxed enough to do the writing activity that you need to do, move slowly and purposefully into that task, keeping your attention focused as much as possible on your breathing to retain your relaxed state of mind.

The Many Uses of Progressive Relaxation

There are dozens of ways that you can use progressive relaxation to your creative benefit. In fact, progressive relaxation is the foundation skill for using the remaining techniques in this book for creativity purposes. Start practicing with the enclosed CD and begin each of the activities outlined in this section with either the full or short programs. The nice thing about progressive relaxation is that you can do it anywhere and anytime, and it gets easier and the results more profound each time you practice with the techniques.

The Writer's Block

Learning to relax is the foundation skill for the creative process. It allows you to access your subconscious mind and bypass the other two elements of the mind: the conscious and preconscious. You can begin to tap into your subconscious mind through relaxation. Most people have forgotten how to relax because of the hectic lifestyle of modern society, but you can learn to relax using the simple tools in this chapter. Remember:

- Relaxation of the body produces alpha brain waves, increasing focus and concentration and stimulating creativity.

- There are two relaxation programs on the enclosed CD: a long program and a short program. Both can help you get into a state of mind that is conducive to creativity.

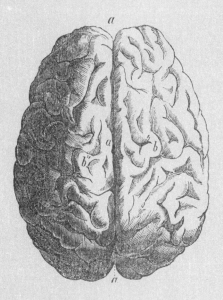

part ii

Accessing Your Subconscious Mind

CHAPTER FIVE

Dream Your
Way to
Creativity

For the writer, dreams are a powerful source of creativity and a venue to problem solving. They are often rich with symbolism, metaphor, and creative inspiration. When you learn to utilize the dream mechanism of subconscious communication, you can use them to generate ideas for plots, create new characters, and get guidance when you are stuck.

What are dreams? Dreams are one way that information passes from the subconscious into the conscious mind and they can help you access your creativity easily and naturally. Your subconscious mind is always alert and constantly thinking—even during sleep—and dreaming allows your subconscious mind to get information into the conscious mind in a way that bypasses attention. This information could be of any variety, such as processing the day's events or generating solutions to problems.

If you think you don't dream, do not be discouraged. Everyone dreams. You are just not consciously remembering what you dreamt about. In fact, it's likely that you already use a simple form of dream communication. You can probably recall a time when someone asked you a question and you replied, "I'll have to sleep on it."

This gave you time to process the situation and make a sound decision. Even though you may not remember having a specific dream related to the question, your subconscious mind did work on the problem while you slept. The techniques in this chapter will allow you to begin remembering your dreams and, as you begin to remember, you can efficiently use the dream mechanism to benefit your writing.

Dreams for Subconscious Access

Learning to remember your dreams is probably the easiest way to access your subconscious mind's creative material. Some people seem to remember their dreams more easily than others. Those who remember their dreams on a regular basis are much more likely to experience vivid dreams that can be used for writing than those who do not remember them. This is logical since the more you remember your dreams, the greater the likelihood that you will have and remember the creative ones.

You remember dreams with your conscious mind by instructing your subconscious mind to provide specific information before you go to sleep and then sometime later, perhaps the next morning or even a few weeks later, the information is received back into consciousness in the form of a dream or dream recall experience. This natural means of subconscious communication is much the same as sending away to a company for information: you write a letter to a company (your subconscious), mail the letter (instruct your subconscious), and wait for a reply (dream recall). Just as in waiting for a reply in the mail, you don't know when the response will arrive, but you know that it will eventually get to you.

Cultivate an Attitude of Expectation

You take the first step to remembering your dreams by expecting to do so. Remember, one of the characteristics of creative people is their expectation to receive guidance from their subconscious mind. Since dreams are a primary way to obtain this guidance, expecting to receive ideas, stories, and creative inspiration from your dreams conveys a message of genuine intent to your subconscious mind that you want this to happen.

The Voice of Experience

"I often work on my stories while I'm sleeping, especially when using cliff-hangers. I'll get my character into a fix that I can't figure a way out of, then I'll go to sleep expecting to dream up the next scene."

—Stephen LaFevers, Electronic Publishing Award finalist author of *Dreams of April Ten*

Subconscious influence is the sum of genuine intent + repetition + burning desire. Using this formula, the simplest way to cultivate an attitude of expectation about remembering your dreams is to tell your subconscious each night before you fall asleep that you will remember your dreams consciously the next day. It may take practice, but over time, this genuine intent, repetition, and desire will lead to an increased rate of dream recall.

Keep a Dream Journal

Keep a dream journal—a physical manifestation of your intention to gain access to your subconscious mind's resources and guidance—beside your bed to record any thoughts you have upon awakening, even if they're limited. You may remember symbols or strange words. Write these down, because over time their meaning may become clear. Writing down your dreams every day allows you to see trends and patterns emerging and reinforces the notion to your subconscious mind that you will remember them. Decorating and personalizing a dream journal gives your dreams a special place to live and creates a feeling of their sacredness.

The Voice of Experience

"During the writing process, I definitely dream about my story and characters. When I'm deep in, they are often the last thing on my mind before sleep and the first thing on it when I awake."

—Kristen Painter

Purchase a blank journal at any office supply store and personalize it in any way that seems right to you. You can use:

- Feathers
- Glitter
- Buttons and thread
- Inspirational words or pictures cut from magazines
- Handwritten notes

- Stickers
- Tissue
- Construction paper
- Anything else that is meaningful to you

While you are decorating the cover, don't censor yourself. Allow whatever images that come into your mind to be your guide for personalizing your dream journal. After you finish, use a special pen for recording your dreams. I like to use a gel pen in an unusual color, such as purple. Keep the journal close by and get in the habit of recording your dreams before you get out of bed. Record the date of each dream so you can track your progress and identify patterns.

Instruct Your Subconscious to Provide a Dream Solution

Thinking about your work-in-progress is often a natural byproduct of spending time with your writing every day. As you begin to focus on your story, it naturally stays in the forefront of your mind, and your subconscious works on it even when you aren't at your desk. It will be with you when you go to bed at night and when you wake up. Because you have been thinking about it all day long, you can instruct your subconscious mind to give you a dream solution prior to falling asleep.

Jacquelyn Mitchard is the *New York Times* bestselling author of *The Deep End of the Ocean*, *Twelve Times Blessed*, and fourteen other novels for adults and children. She explains that instructing her subconscious mind to give her a solution to a plot problem through dreams is a common practice for her. Notice how she actively directs her subconscious mind prior to sleep by giving it highly specific instructions related to her current work-in-progress. She says, "I have definitely used sleep to solve plot problems that seemed hopelessly tangled in waking work. In fact, I have sought those dream interventions, which I think of as my unconscious talking to my conscious, by telling myself as I go to sleep, 'I'm going to be with Claire and Blaine, or whoever my characters are, now.'" This type of fluidity between the writing and sleep states occurs naturally when you become engrossed in your project. Often, writers find that even when they are not writing, their characters are still with them and the story lingers in the background of their mind. This sets up a process by which the sleep state is ripe to provide dreams that enhance the storytelling.

The Voice of Experience

"Often, the last thing I'm thinking about before sleep is my story. I think about where I am in the plot, what needs to happen next, that kind of thing. If I'm having a problem with a plot twist or the resolution, then I may go so far as to focus on it before sleep, telling myself to dream up a solution."

—Bonnie Edwards, author of *Midnight Confessions* and other novels

Steep Yourself in Your Writing

Requesting a dream solution works best when you "steep" yourself in your writing before going to bed. This means that you immerse yourself in your story right before going to sleep and allow its elements to infuse your subconscious mind. This is like priming the pump; you are feeding material into your subconscious mind and anticipating that you will get back ideas and solutions for the next writing session. It's a common technique of successful authors. "I will steep myself in the book before I go to bed, read over chapters, look at character outlines, and just think about it as I'm going to sleep," says Berta Platas, author of *Lucky Chica* and other novels. Platas, who keeps a dream journal beside her bed, points out that even if she does not remember the actual dream, she is always ready to go forward with the writing after immersing herself in the project the night before.

You do not have to read your entire manuscript or all of your research materials in order to use this exercise. Simply gather up any material from your work-in-progress that you want your subconscious to help you with that night. Ensure that you will have a few minutes of quiet and solitude to read over your material. This may mean reviewing your outline, reading character profiles in order to flesh them out, reading over some research notes or the draft of your essay, or anything else that is related to your current project. Give this portion of your writing project your full, undivided attention for several minutes. Absorb the material. Let it soak into your mind. Think about it. Ask questions in your mind about any areas that you need help with.

When you feel ready, put the materials away and go directly to sleep. As you drift off, mentally review what you just read. Ask your subconscious to give you a dream that will provide whatever you need next: the following scene, a solution to a plot problem, a character's next action, a way to break out of writer's block, or a fresh idea. Ask for whatever you need your subconscious to provide guidance on. For ease of recall, it's important to only ask for one thing per dream request. Remember to demonstrate an attitude of expectation by keeping your dream journal and pen nearby to record ideas that come to you upon awakening.

Ask for Editing Help

You can ask for a dream solution to anything writing related, even minor problems like editing. This is a common technique for successful writers. Even if you do not remember the details of the dream the next day, usually a solution will be there. This technique allows you to resolve troublesome areas of the work-in-progress that you had difficulty overcoming the day before.

The Voice of Experience

"I will put a problem in my head when I go to sleep. My brain is processing all this stuff at an underlying level. When I'm awake, I can pull it out and have it be fully formed."

—Judi McCoy, award-winning author of *Hounding the Pavement* and other novels.

I have used dream solution work with my own writing. For example, the night before I handed in the manuscript for my previous book, *Time to Write*, I reread the entire draft. Before falling asleep, I asked my subconscious mind to alert me the next morning to any errors in the copy. When I woke up, I immediately pictured three misspelled words within the body of a 60,000-word document. I opened the document and found the errors in the exact sections that my subconscious had indicated they would be in, which allowed me to make the corrections before turning in the final copy to my editor.

Get a clear picture on what it is you need help with; the more specific the better. For example, I asked to be alerted to any typographical errors in the manuscript. Pose the question to your subconscious mind right before falling asleep. You can write this question down, ask it out loud, or visualize it in your mind. Be specific and clear about what you need, and be ready the next morning with a notebook and pen to record any answers that come to you.

If the answer does not come the next day, continue to pose your question night after night. It may take some time before you receive an answer, and sometimes the insight will come when your brain is in an alpha or theta mode, when you are driving, sitting in a boring meeting at work, or exercising. Have an attitude of expectation that the solution will come to you and it will.

Record Middle-of-the-Night Material

Rapid-eye-movement (REM) sleep is the time when you dream the most, and the most vividly. Since creativity is at a peak during REM sleep, you want to capture as much dream material as possible during this phase. A good way to do this is to get in the habit of writing down whatever you are thinking whenever you wake up in the middle of the night to use the restroom, get a snack, or on those occasions when you have trouble sleeping.

Most people enter the first REM cycle about seventy to ninety minutes after first falling asleep, and will have three to five episodes of REM sleep each night, each one lasting about an hour. REM sleep is useful for writers because of the richness of the dreams that occur during this time. In one study, people were awakened during REM and non–REM sleep and asked to describe their dreams. The dreams they described during REM sleep were much more vivid and creative than those that occurred at non–REM times of the night.

Be sure to place a pen and your dream journal by your bed so you can find them in the dark. Before you fall asleep, ask your subconscious mind to remind you to write down your dreams whenever you wake up during the night. When you do wake up, immediately write down anything that comes to mind, even if it seems like total nonsense at the time. Do not bother to turn on the light, just scribble away.

The Voice of Experience

"There's no way of knowing how much subconscious work is going on while I sleep, work that only bears fruit when I'm awake and pondering the problem."

—Tess Gerritsen

Some writers leave their computers on at night and whenever they spontaneously wake up, they get up and go to the computer and write. Fran McNabb, author of *Once in a Half Moon*, does this to ensure that dream material will not be lost the next day. She says, "I have gotten up in the middle of the night to go to my computer to finish a scene or to write something new. I know I have to write it down before it slips away."

Write as Much as Your Subconscious Gives You

In addition to techniques for remembering your dreams, there are ways to solicit guidance and feedback from your subconscious through sleep. Writers commonly write until they reach an obstacle, go to sleep, and then find they have enough information to continue the story the next day. It appears that just the act of sleeping, even simply taking a short nap, can resolve a writer's problems.

"When I'm working on a new story idea, the key is to sit down every day and write as much as I know. My subconscious works when I'm not at the computer, but it only tells me what it has worked out when I sit down to write," says Robin Wells, award-winning author of *Between the Sheets* and other novels. "The same thing with scenes; every day, I write as much as I know. When I don't know what comes next, I stop writing. When I come back to the story, I know what comes next."

Remember, our minds are in a constant state of consciousness. During sleep, the stream of consciousness switches from conscious, linear thinking to subconscious, nonlinear thinking. This is why solutions that are not obvious to the waking mind become so vivid and obvious during sleep.

I used this method of prompting the subconscious to give me scenes piece by piece while writing a short story that came to me in a dream. Other than the initial dream that gave me the core of the story, the character's name, and that she was in a strange town for a reason known only to her, I had no clue what the story was about or where it was leading. Each night before going to sleep, I would tell my subconscious, "In the morning, provide me with the next scene in the story."

Each morning I wrote the next section of the story that had come to me when I woke up. I did not recall dreaming about it, but I knew upon awakening what was supposed to happen next. That first dream planted a seed that over the next two months became a 9,000-word short story.

This prompting technique is useful regarding your writing aspirations, too. If you want to know if you should submit your work to a particular agent, say or write something like, "Subconscious, tell me in the morning if Agent X is a good match for me."

If you want to know if a writing conference will be worth your investment of time, say or write, "Subconscious, in the morning tell me if I should attend this writing workshop."

If you want to know if you should focus on writing fiction rather than nonfiction, ask or write, "Subconscious, lead me to know if I should focus on fiction or nonfiction."

Expect to receive an answer in the form of words that pop into your mind, a mental image, or a hunch.

Famous Writers Who Used Their Dreams

Using dreams to inform and inspire the creative writing process was a common technique of writers in the past. Robert Louis Stevenson—who had vivid dreams throughout his childhood—is famously known for his use of dreams for his writing material. Many times these dreams were so real that he would awaken in another part of the room, trembling with fright. He once wrote that the startling difference between his awake and sleeping selves was the basis for the story behind *The Strange Story of Dr. Jekyll and Mr. Hyde*, which he wrote in ten weeks after having the dream that prompted it. In his dream, he was standing outside a window, watching as a man pursued by the police for a hideous crime drank a substance that caused a physical transformation.

However, most of Stevenson's dreams were pleasant and useful to him. So thankful was he to receive his writing material this way that he called his dreams his "brownies" and his "little people," and credited them with providing him with all of his novels, chapter by chapter. He eagerly anticipated his nightly sleep and referred to his dreams as the "stage" of his mind. Stevenson would often awake in a state of euphoria, thrilled because he had gotten the idea for his next book or the next chapter for his work-in-progress.

An important aspect of Stevenson's use of dream material is the fact that he *expected* his dreams to provide him with story ideas. He frequently went to sleep anticipating a dream that would inspire his next book.

Napoleon Hill, the founder of positive thinking and ways to effectively program the subconscious mind for self-improvement, is another author who used the dream mechanism for writing assistance. He relates how he solved a problem regarding his popular self-help book *Think and Grow Rich* by programming his subconscious before sleep. Hill had written the book but was having trouble coming up with a title for it. However, the publisher was eager to go to print. When Hill still hadn't presented a title, the publisher told him that if he didn't come up with a title by the next day, the book would be called *Use Your Noodle and Make a Boodle*. This horrified Hill as he felt his reputation would be ruined. So, using the techniques he had written about, he asked his subconscious mind to give him a title and then went to sleep. The next morning he woke up with *Think and Grow Rich* running through his head, a title that went on to sell millions of copies.

Contemporary Writers

Contemporary writers use dreams as a source of story ideas and plots, too. Award-winning novelist Debra Mullins, author of *The Night Before the Wedding*, got the plot for that book from a dream. Raven Hart, author of *The Vampire Seduction* and other novels, says that the plot for her first published book also came to her full-blown in a dream. All she had to do was write it.

Even if the plot does not come fully formed, there is usually enough information given in a dream upon which to build a book. "The theme of my first book *Take Me* came from a dream," says Bella Andre, author of *Wild Heat* and other novels. "I'd dreamed of a man and woman who had known each other for a while. She'd been in love with him forever, but he'd never noticed her until one day, the tables turned and he couldn't get enough of her and wanted her to be his. In my dream he said, 'You're mine, all mine,' and that's what I titled the draft."

Many authors receive guidance for writer's block in their dreams. "The most common experience for me is solving plot problems in my dreams," says Allison Brennan, *New York Times* bestselling author of *Sudden Death* and other novels. Brennan explains that the solutions to her plot problems always happen after sleeping, and even though she may not recall the details of the actual dream, she does remember the solution and it frees up her writing the next day.

Learning to remember your dreams and using pre-sleep subconscious instructions are effective ways to boost your creativity and work out problems with your writing. Dreams are a common way that successful authors get story ideas, and you can, too. The more you practice remembering your dreams, the more you will remember them. Cultivate an attitude of expectation and the dream solutions will come!

The Writer's Block

Dreams are a common way for information to pass from the subconscious into the conscious mind; many writers use the dream process to access their creativity easily and naturally. Dreaming is the easiest way to tap into your subconscious, and a common way that many writers get their story ideas. Robert Louis Stevenson got so many ideas from his dreams that he called them his "brownies."

If you have trouble remembering your dreams, try these tips:

- Record your dreams. Just the act of writing down any snippets of dreams will encourage retention.

- Decorate a dream journal. This gives your dreams a special place to live; it marks those dreams as separate and apart from the daily routine of life, which serves as a reminder to your subconscious about their importance. It also sends a concrete message to your subconscious mind that you want to remember your dreams.

- Read your current work-in-progress just before going to sleep and ask your subconscious mind to provide you with the answer to a question about your story, the next scene, or the next major plot point.

CHAPTER SIX

The *Creative*
Pre-sleep
State

There is a phase of sleep that can be highly beneficial to your writing because it puts you in direct contact with your subconscious mind. This contact happens spontaneously every night, and all you have to do is learn to capitalize on its creative benefits. This phase of sleep is called the hypnagogic state, and it occurs in the minutes just before falling asleep and right before waking up. It's a state similar to hypnosis that you can learn to use for writing benefit because, unlike other sleep states, it is characterized by a brief period of altered consciousness.

A Short but Intensely Creative Period

Researchers who have studied the hypnagogic state found that people perceive things in unusual or altered ways while in this state. For instance, ideas that under ordinary conditions have no association are perceived as being connected in this state. Solid objects may be perceived as sound or flashes of light. Some people report hearing or seeing things that do not exist. Images become vivid and intensely real. It is similar to having a dream while you are still semi-awake. But because it happens quickly, much of that creative material is lost. However, writers can learn to expand upon and stay functionally in this state, bringing that material into the conscious mind for creative purposes.

The Voice of Experience

"I do sometimes dream about my characters and my plot and occasionally get some new ideas in that half-asleep time just before waking up."

—Barbara Freethy, *USA Today* bestselling author of *Silent Fall* and other novels

This in-between state occurs as the brain begins exhibiting alpha and theta waves, indicating increased relaxation of the body, which in turn sets up access to the subconscious mind. Many people experience spontaneous bouts of creativity during these times. You've had these types of experiences, too. When you are falling asleep, you may hear your name being called or see a flash of light in the room. Perhaps a vivid scenario passes through your mind that seems bizarre and whimsical. This is the hypnagogic state.

Writers and the Hypnagogic State

Several famous writers throughout history have capitalized on the hypnagogic state to benefit their writing. One example is Mary Shelley, the author of the classic novel *Frankenstein*. On a rainy winter afternoon, Shelley dozed on the couch in front of a roaring fire. As she was dropping off to sleep, she had what she described later as a disturbing vision of a man huddled over a pale monster that was stirring to life. She used this vision to create her famous story.

The Voice of Experience

"I woke up in the middle of the night seeing the entire scene."

—Dianna Love, *New York Times* bestselling author of *Phantom in the Night* and other novels

The famous inventor Thomas Edison frequently used the hypnagogic state to solve problems. When confronted with a dilemma with one of his inventions, he would deliberately induce the hypnagogic state by lying down on the table in his lab and dozing in a state of half-wakefulness while focusing on his problem. In order to stay in the state, he held two steel balls over metal plates. Whenever he started to doze off, his hands would relax and he would drop the balls. The loud noise would awaken him, enabling him to easily recall what was passing through his mind in the moments before sleep and thereby securing the solution to his problem.

Julia Ward Howe is another example. She wrote the famous song *Battle Hymn of the Republic* in its entirety in the predawn hours of November 19, 1861. Howe, a published author, had seen weary Union soldiers straggle by her hotel window one night when she was traveling. Howe watched as the soldiers tramped by, their boots making a methodical stamping sound, lights from the hotel flashing against their bayonets. The sight triggered the memory of a recent conversation she had had with the Reverend James Freeman Clarke, who had asked her to write an inspirational camp song for the Union soldiers. Howe had agreed, but so far nothing had come to her.

The Voice of Experience

"I've seen whole scenes in those last drowsy moments before I fall asleep or wake up."

—Kerrelyn Sparks

Exhausted from her trip, Howe went to bed with the image of the soldiers and the desire to write the song fresh on her mind. It's likely that the methodical tramping noise from the soldiers' boots in addition to the flashing light on their weapons induced the hypnagogic state because Howe awakened suddenly in the predawn hours and, later barely remembered doing what came next. She sat at her desk and began scribbling—in the dark and with her eyes closed—the verses that were presenting themselves intact in her mind. When she was done writing, she went back to bed.

Rising at her normal hour, she discovered the *Battle Hymn of the Republic* on her desk. Howe was so pleased with the poem that she only changed four words. Later she would often state that she did not write the poem, that it wrote itself. Howe probably woke up in the hypnagogic state, composed the entire song, and never got back to a normal state of consciousness before returning to bed. When she woke up she didn't realize what she had done until she saw the writing.

Howe's case demonstrates how access to the subconscious via the hypnagogic state often works; in her situation, a seed was planted in her subconscious mind by the Reverend Clarke's request for the song that later sprouted as creative inspiration in the hypnagogic state.

How to Use the Hypnagogic State

You have the ability to enter the hypnagogic state at will. Sasha White, the author of *Wicked* and other novels, purposefully uses this naturally occurring state to come up with fresh ideas or work through plot problems. "I lie down and close my eyes and think, 'Okay what would happen next?' Then that's when the ideas come. The trick is remembering those ideas when you wake up," she says. Similar to White, you can learn to capitalize on the moments before dozing off to benefit your own writing, and there are ways to ensure that you will remember what came to you during this state when you return to normal consciousness.

The Voice of Experience

"If I can awaken slowly, with no interruptions or urgent need to get up, and just drift for a while, my mind comes up with the most marvelous things which I then jot down."

—Lisa Hendrix, author of *Immortal Outlaw* and other novels

With practice, you can learn to stay in the hypnagogic state before falling asleep and also when waking up. Like White, you can induce it when necessary to assist you with your writing endeavors. To begin, experiment with the hypnagogic state when you are already rested in order to avoid slipping into deep sleep right away. A good time is on a weekend or on a morning that you have no pressing obligations. Don't be discouraged if you have trouble staying in the hypnagogic state. As with all of these techniques, it takes practice and patience. Over time, you will be able to increase the amount of time you can stay in this state without falling asleep. For the best results, ensure that you will not be disturbed for twenty to thirty minutes so you can totally relax. Then use the following methods to stay in the hypnagogic state.

Hold Marbles over Ceramic Bowls

This method is similar to the one Edison used when he cat-napped while holding metal balls over plates. Lie down on a single bed or cot and place two ceramic bowls on the floor. Hold marbles over the bowls after you lie down. You can also lay back in a comfortable chair, positioning the marbles over the bowls while resting your arms on the armrests.

Use one of the relaxation exercises on the CD to begin, then let your mind drift as if you were about to doze off. Don't worry about falling asleep; the tension in your hands required to hold the marbles will keep you semi-alert. If you do fall asleep, your hands will relax and you will drop the marbles, which will wake you up.

As you begin to shift into a semi-asleep state, focus on your work-in-progress. Mentally ask any questions that you have about the writing. As you begin to drift into a semi-asleep state, you should start to get images, sounds, or flashes of insight.

If you drop the marbles, simply start again as many times as you wish.

When you get tired or want to quit, lie quietly to allow yourself to return to full consciousness before sitting up. Then record all of your observations and experiences in a notebook or recorder. Do not analyze or judge the material. Over time, unusual scenes or symbols may become clearer to you, or you might see patterns emerge that are useful to you in your writing.

Hold One Arm Straight Up while Dozing

This technique is based on the work of Dr. Raymond Moody, a psychiatrist who has studied the link between the subconscious mind and creativity. It is easy to do in bed before you go to sleep at night. Simply hold one arm straight up in the air after you lie down. This has the same effect as holding the marbles over the bowls; the muscle tension required to hold your arm up will keep you on the verge of consciousness. If you do fall asleep, your arm will fall and wake you up, allowing you to record your hypnagogic images and insights.

Keep your notebook nearby to write down your flashes of insight and bursts of creativity when your falling arm awakens you. The more you practice this exercise, the easier it will become.

Stay in Your Pajamas

The above methods induce hypnagogia when you are falling asleep. A good way to take advantage of the hypnagogic state right after waking up is to stay in your pajamas.

Changing into clothes immediately upon rising jars your mind and sends a signal to your brain that it's time to wake up and get on with the day. Over the years, getting dressed for the day becomes a conditioned response that alerts your brain to shift into delta brain wave mode. Staying in your pajamas minimizes this response and keeps your brain in an alpha state, thereby creating a mind state conducive to creativity.

Brenda Ueland talks about this strategy in her classic book *If You Want to Write*. Ueland suggests that you should go straight to your desk and start writing as soon as you wake up. Open your computer file and start pouring the words out without censorship. Do not edit what you wrote the day before. Do not do research. Do not check e-mail, make a phone call, or review the sports scores on ESPN first. If you need coffee, set it up the night before so that all you have to do is grab the freshly brewed pot as you walk by. Simply sit down at your desk and start writing whatever comes to mind. This will help you take advantage of the hypnagogic state.

Remember, learning to use this naturally occurring brain state by employing the techniques discussed in this chapter will enrich your writing and lead to enhanced creativity. The techniques are easy to learn, and the more you practice the better you will get at staying in the hypnagogic state. Your writing creativity will certainly be enriched by learning to use a mind state that is already as natural to you as breathing.

The Writer's Block

The hypnagogic state is an intensely fertile creative period that occurs in the moments right before you fall asleep and in the drowsy moments before you awaken fully. It occurs naturally to everyone every day. Many writers and creators, including Thomas Edison, used this spontaneous phase of sleep for creative purposes. You too can capitalize on this time by intentionally staying in the state for as long as possible. The trick is to remember what occurs during this creative pre-sleep state, so try these tips with a notebook and pen beside you:

- Hold marbles over ceramic plates as you doze off; the muscle tension required to hold the marbles will keep you on the edge of consciousness.

- Fall asleep while holding one arm straight up. When your arm falls, immediately record whatever was going on in your mind.

CHAPTER SEVEN

Seeing Your
Subconscious Mind's
Images

D id you know that, with practice, you can actually see the images of your subconscious mind? That's right. An unconventional but fun way to access your subconscious mind for creative material is to employ a reflective surface such as a mirror, crystal, or pond and gaze into it in a relaxed, meditative state. (Please note that the terms "subconscious projection" and "mirror gazing" are, for our purposes, interchangeable.)

Using a reflective surface as an aid for visualizing images from the subconscious mind is an ancient practice. Unlike the cartoon character of a gypsy in gaudy scarves leaning over a crystal ball and predicting an innocent victim's gloomy future, the use of reflective surfaces to gain access to the subconscious is a legitimate practice, one that has a documented place in history. Native Americans used variations of it for divination, as did the ancient Greeks and Egyptians. Looking into a reflective surface for images from the subconscious mind as a way of gaining guidance and insight into one's life was also a popular pastime around the turn of the twentieth century, when it was often used as a parlor game. In fact, Sir Walter Scott wrote about the technique of using a mirror for subconscious projection in his book *My Aunt Margaret's Mirror.*

Throughout history, many items have been used as the object on which to project the images from the subconscious mind. These include a pool of ink in the hand, a goblet of wine, or water in a dark bowl. The practice of gazing into a goblet of water with a sheen of olive oil across the surface is done today in the Middle East and is considered a part of the culture.

More conventional items for gazing include clear quartz crystals, a small still pond (aptly called a reflecting pond), a reconstituted clear quartz crystal ball, or a fishbowl filled with water. The easiest item to use when learning subconscious projection is a mirror, since mirrors are readily available. A mirror is what you will learn to use in this chapter.

The Voice of Experience

"Leave yourself open to letting your imagination go wild."

—Allison Brennan

Some people have a knack for subconscious projection and will see images in the mirror right away. However, most everyone can learn to actually see the images from the subconscious mind on the surface of the mirror with enough practice. This is a great way to access your subconscious creativity, gain insight into stories and characters, and get fresh ideas for your creative writing sessions.

How Will This Help Your Writing?

The technique of projecting subconscious images onto a reflective surface is highly useful for writers. There are many ways you can use this process to aid your creative writing, including:

- *Flesh out scenes.* Since many authors get their story ideas in the form of intact picture scenes like trailers from a movie, mirror gazing can be used to enhance or get details about those scenes.
- *Create characters.* Mirror gazing can be used to picture details about a character that you are having difficulty pinning down—the color of a person's eyes, for example, or what they are wearing at a certain time in history.
- *Develop plot.* Let's say you keep picturing the same scene over and over in your mind, and your characters are acting in ways that are totally unlike them. You like this direction for the novel but you have no idea what should happen that leads up to that scene. Mirror gazing helps you communicate with your subconscious mind in order to get direction on what came before this scene.
- *Get important symbols that are helpful to you personally.* Because the subconscious sometimes thinks in symbols, symbols may emerge from the subconscious mind onto the reflective surface. These images are usually important to the person doing the gazing and can be interpreted for guidance and direction in a story line.

Subconscious Projection Techniques for Creativity

Learning to use subconscious projection techniques is something that takes time, and the easiest way to begin is to start with a mirror in your home. This can be a mirror hanging on the wall or a stand-alone mirror used for applying makeup. The only requirement is that it is large enough that you can see images in it. (A mirror that comes with a cosmetics compact is not big enough.)

1. First, eliminate all distractions. Set aside time when you can be undisturbed for about an hour. Then set up the area. Drape the walls around the mirror with black fabric, using something lightweight, such as cotton. Hang the cloth behind the mirror, as well as behind your head so the surface of the mirror is black. Place a comfortable chair in front of the mirror. If you are using a handheld mirror, lay the fabric across your lap and behind you, so that the surface reflecting on the mirror is black.

2. Next, set up a light source. Candlelight lends an aura of mystery to the process, but to avoid the risk of fire, use an electric candle or an electric night light. Put the light source behind you, and darken the rest of the room.

3. Get into a comfortable position. If the mirror is on the wall, it should be positioned so that you have to gaze up at it slightly. You want to be able to see into it, but you do not want to see your own reflection. It may take a few minutes to adjust the position of your mirror and your chair.

4. Use the progressive relaxation script on the CD to get into a quiet, focused, relaxed state. Then gaze *into* the mirror, as if you were looking at something far away. Turn off your anti-writer and have an attitude of expectation. Expect to see something in the mirror—this could be color, light, something that looks like smoke, or actual images. It may seem as if space opens up behind the mirror and you could step through it. Whatever appears, just go with it. It may take a while for something to come. It's important to have patience and concentrate on relaxing. Don't think, judge, analyze, or try to interpret your experience while it's happening.

5. When you start to feel tired, turn on the lights and allow yourself to slowly come back to a normal state of consciousness. Then record in a notebook the images and insights that appeared. Even if the images or symbols do not seem significant at the time, it's possible they will mean something to you later on, and you want to have a recording of them.

After a certain amount of practice, you reach a point with this technique where the images move so freely that it becomes like watching a movie. Because of this spontaneous effect, you can use it as an aid to your writing. Any time you need information about your plot, your characters, or happenings in your story, you can turn to subconscious image projection for guidance. Before the session begins, ask your subconscious mind to show you the next scene, a new character, or give you guidance about anything related to your writing. Then proceed with the session as indicated above and allow images to flow. It's important to trust the process and record whatever appears in your notebook.

The Voice of Experience

"Once you find what works for you then you enter a new phase in your life and you have to start all over again. Being creative isn't a fixed state."

—Susan Elizabeth Phillips, *New York Times* bestselling author of *What I Did for Love* and other novels

It's important to note that everyone's experience with this technique is different. Just as your subconscious mind is unique, the images that it projects will be unique, too. Whatever your experience, the images your subconscious mind offers up will be useful to you even if it does not seem so at the time. Recording your experiences over time will help you see patterns and aid you in making sense of them.

Famous Authors Use Subconscious Projection for Creativity

Many famous writers, including Jane Austen, have used mirror gazing to help them gain access to subconscious images. The Austen family had a big polished metal screen in their living room, and she would gaze and watch the visions and stories going by.

Robert Louis Stevenson also used gazing to gain access to his subconscious for writing material. Stevenson was very in tune with his subconscious processes and relied heavily on them for material for his work. In addition to using his dreams as discussed in Chapter 5, Stevenson also used various gazing techniques—like gazing into a wine-filled goblet—to get ideas and inspiration for his books.

My Experience with Mirror Gazing

I first learned of this technique from Dr. Raymond Moody, psychiatrist and author of several books on the subject. I want to share my experience of learning mirror gazing because it helped me see how easy it is to access my subconscious mind using this technique. My experience demonstrates that the images and sensations were being pulled out of my subconscious mind; I wasn't thinking of the particular things that came up when I entered the experience. It is a strong example of the types of creative and unusual experiences you can have with mirror gazing that you may not be able to have otherwise, and it illustrates how this technique can stimulate creativity and be an aid in the creative writing process.

At Dr. Moody's office, I was directed to a small room designed as the mirror gazing room or what he calls his "Theatre of the Mind." The room had a low sloping roof and was draped in black fabric. There was a low comfortable chair below a large gold-framed mirror on the wall. A white noise machine and an electric candle behind the chair completed the furnishings.

The Voice of Experience

"They are all mental tricks,
but why question them if they work?"

—Jacquelyn Mitchard

After getting physically relaxed, I gazed into the mirror. Approximately thirty minutes later, it seemed as if space or a room opened up behind the mirror. I had the distinct feeling that if I got up, I could step into the mirror and be somewhere else. At other times the scene would change and it seemed as if the mirror became a window through which I was peering out into a dark, starry night. I saw shadows and movement of light in the mirror. There was bright light at the edges of the mirror that seemed to shift and grow in intensity. At one point it seemed that there was a tablet or rolled parchment paper inside the mirror and that the lower edge of it was poking out at me. I saw a few gray tendrils of smoke coming out of the left side of the mirror.

I also experienced a lot of physical sensations. There was pressure in my head around the eyes and forehead and temple area, and it felt as though there was a string in my solar plexus that was being pulled out. There was a rolling or circling sensation in my throat, near the thyroid.

Toward the end of my hour, the mirror became a big white square that moved from inside the mirror to the outside. It overtook the frame. At the same time, my body started vibrating. It got more and more intense and I felt like I was revving up to take off out of the chair. I was in a trance yet there was a small portion of my mind that seemed outside my body. I was completely lucid and knew exactly what was going on, yet I was observing myself from outside my body.

After taking a short break, I went back in for another session. The second time I also saw the white parchment paper with the lower edge coming out of the mirror. It again seemed as if space opened up behind the mirror and I could step through it and be somewhere else. I saw two faint images of old white doors that were pointed at the top, typical of those seen in ancient churches. Toward the end of this session I heard music that sounded like chimes.

All the physical sensations and phenomena that I was experiencing during my session — such as hearing chimes — were the personal manifestations of my subconscious mind. Even though this was my first attempt, and I had very interesting results, please understand that your experience may be completely different from mine. Everyone's mind is different, and the manifestations of your mind will be different from mine and others. What's important is that you relax and go with the flow. Simply watch and observe your own mind. You will have full use of your faculties at all times throughout the process.

How I Use Mirror Gazing to Help with Writing

After this interesting experience, I began to use subconscious reflection techniques at home on a regular basis to help with my writing and creative output. Instead of a mirror, I use a reconstituted quartz crystal ball. These are readily available online and affordable.

Since learning the practice I've seen an increase in the vividness of my dreams and have experienced fewer writing blocks. My writing seems to flow better. It's as if a channel between my conscious mind and subconscious creativity has been opened. For example, I am not one of those writers who typically has a constant stream of ideas for books and stories. I usually have to work to generate topics to write about. However, the day after I have a mirror gazing session, I have noticed that flashes of inspiration and ideas come to me spontaneously much more frequently.

The routine has also created a sense of being more in touch with inner portions of myself the more I practice; writing feels more organic to me after a mirror gazing session. It's as if I connect with my subconscious mind in the act of writing more easily after a round of mirror gazing. Remember, the key with using subconscious projection techniques is to have an open mind. It may seem far-fetched, but mirror gazing is documented, time-tested, and a reliable means of communicating with the subconscious mind. Some people have a knack for it, and you just may be one of them. I hope you will give it a try, and when you do please write to me and let me know how it works for you. My e-mail address is included at the end of the book.

The Writer's Block

Mirror gazing, or subconscious mind projection, is an ancient practice of seeing images from the subconscious on a reflective surface such as a mirror, a still pond, or a clear crystal. Watching elements in your subconscious mind is a skill that can be learned through the easy practice of mirror gazing. This technique helps to open a channel between the conscious and the subconscious and stimulates spontaneous creativity. To practice subconscious mind projection, you should:

- Designate a space in your home to set up a mirror gazing area. This should include a low, comfortable chair, a large mirror or handheld mirror, a soft light behind the chair, and a white noise machine.

- Get relaxed and gaze into the mirror, as if staring off into the distance. You can simply watch whatever comes up, or you can pose a question; make notes about your experience when you are done.

CHAPTER EIGHT

An Easy

Subconscious Communication

Technique

T he subconscious mind is the most powerful computer system in existence. It has a constant stream of data input from the senses and stores everything. With your home computer, you have input sources such as your mouse, keyboard, scanner and the Internet connection. However, what would happen if you had no monitor or printer? The computer would still be collecting data but you couldn't benefit from it because you have no output device. All the data would be trapped.

The subconscious mind works the same way. To retrieve information from which you can consciously benefit, you need an output device that can connect to the subconscious mind— something to allow you to ask questions of your subconscious mind and get a "printout" of the answers. Fortunately, gaining access to that creative portion of your mind is as simple as using a pendulum made from a piece of sewing thread and a flat #10 washer that you can purchase at any home supply store. Communication using this pendulum is an effective and easy way to gain access to your subconscious creativity, and to get your subconscious mind to help you in a very direct way with your writing.

How It Works

The pendulum is the easiest concrete method to communicate with your subconscious mind because you are making use of ideomotor responses—unconscious physical processes in the body controlled by the subconscious mind not dependent on conscious mind direction. The most obvious ideomotor responses are the ones controlled by your automatic nervous system that we have already discussed: your heartbeat, breathing, body temperature, blood circulation, and so forth. These unconscious body mechanisms are controlled by the subconscious mind without any conscious effort on your part.

The Voice of Experience

"I like to believe in the magic of writing and know, or at least hope, that some of the best stuff comes organically."

—Bella Andre

Necessary adjustments in your body's functioning are made automatically and constantly by the subconscious mind. For example, when you are exercising and your body needs more oxygen, your heart beats faster, your respiration increases, and your blood vessels expand to circulate more oxygen through your system. When you're done exercising, your heart rate slows, your respiration decreases, and your circulatory system reduces the flow of blood through your body. Perspiration automatically cools your body. When you are reading a book and you suddenly look up into the distance, your eyes refocus automatically. All of these things are ideomotor responses. None of them require any conscious intention on your part; the subconscious does it all automatically.

The mechanism of the pendulum operates on the same principle, except it amplifies small subconscious movements so they can be seen. A famous example of using a pendulum to amplify movements that can't be seen or felt is the Foucault pendulum displayed in the Smithsonian's National Museum of American History. This pendulum demonstrates the rotation of the earth, a movement that we can't see or feel, but that we know happens on a continual basis. French physicist Jean Foucault used this pendulum in 1851 as the first satisfactory demonstration of the earth's rotation using a laboratory apparatus rather than astronomical observations.

Our use of the pendulum also measures small movements originating from the subconscious mind. The subconscious controls our involuntary muscles all the time, but can also control the voluntary ones. To communicate with the subconscious using the pendulum, the subconscious mind controls the muscles of the hand. The movements are tiny but the pendulum amplifies them so they can be seen more clearly. We get the subconscious mind to move the pendulum to establish a yes/no/maybe code.

Setting Up a Code

The following method of pendulum communication is based on the work of Robert M. Stone, MS, an expert in the field of subconscious mind communication and author of the enclosed CD.

The first step in using the pendulum method is to make your pendulum. To make your pendulum, tie a flat #10 washer to the end of heavy-duty sewing thread. Then sit at a table or chair with armrests. Place a notebook and pen nearby, then hold the thread between your thumb and forefinger with the washer hanging down. Rest your elbow on the table or the arm of a chair, allowing the washer to hang down about an inch above the table. This will ensure that you get a good swing. Let your arm relax and gaze at the weight, *not* your hand.

Next, you need to set up a code so your subconscious mind can give you information using autonomic muscle responses. The code consists of yes, no, and maybe. Yes and no responses are straightforward; you will ask a question and get a yes or no in return. (We'll talk in just a minute about how to recognize the responses.) The maybe response indicates that the question was not phrased in such a way that you can get a clear yes or no response. Most people are used to answering multifaceted questions, which require interpretation and cannot be answered with a simple yes or no. If you get a maybe answer when using the pendulum, you need to rephrase the question in more straightforward terms.

Next you need to get the directions for the possible three responses (yes, no, maybe) from your subconscious mind. The potential movements of the pendulum to indicate these responses are back and forth, side-to-side, or clockwise and counterclockwise. To get your responses, hold the pendulum above the table, look at the weight, and say or think, "Subconscious mind, select a movement for yes."

Think or say this over and over while you continue to gaze at the weight. Do not pay any attention to what your hand is doing. Repeat the question until you begin to see a movement. The more you repeat the question the stronger the movement will become. In a few minutes, you should see the direction that your subconscious mind swings the pendulum to indicate "yes." Write this down in your notebook so that you will remember it.

Stop the movement of the pendulum, and then determine the movement for "no" and "maybe" in the same way. Keep your gaze on the weight and say or think the question repeatedly until you get a strong movement from the pendulum. Write each of the directions down so that you won't forget them when you use the pendulum in the future.

Once you have established your code, the door to communication with your subconscious mind is open.

Using the Pendulum

After you have established your answer code, you need to write down some questions. By writing down the question first, you'll see if it can be answered with a yes or no response and can change it accordingly. You want to keep up with the answers, so leave a space on your paper to record them.

When you have your questions written down and are ready to begin, let your arm relax and hold the pendulum above the table or the arm of your chair. Stop the pendulum from swinging and gaze at the weight steadily while you ask your subconscious mind a question. For example, let's say you want some guidance on whether or not you should attend a particular writing conference. You would ask, "Subconscious mind, should I attend this writing conference?" Mentally or verbally ask the question over and over; this is important because instead of thinking of an answer to your question, you want your mind to be occupied with asking the question to eliminate conscious mind interference with the answer.

The Voice of Experience

"When you're in creative mode you're open to everything that's going on around you, whether you know it or not."

—Cathy Maxwell

Repeat the question as you watch the pendulum, not your hand. It's important that you focus on the question and not attempt to think up an answer. Since you have the question written down on paper, you can read it if it will help you focus.

As you practice, you will notice that there is a bit of a pause, then a little bit of movement from the weight that will get stronger the longer you concentrate on the question. Eventually the weight will swing in one of the three directions, indicating yes, no, or maybe. Whenever you get a maybe response, try to simplify the question. If you get an answer you did not expect, ask follow-up questions to flesh out the entire picture.

Example: Using the Pendulum

Let's say that you are writing a novel and have come to a sticking point in your plot. You have been working on a particular chapter for weeks and cannot get the story to flow. You have an idea that adding another character to the story might help, but you want to query your subconscious mind first to see if this is the right direction to take with your book.

Sit at your desk or chair with the pendulum, pad, and pen nearby. Get relaxed, and then begin asking your questions.

Remember to think only of your question, not about what you believe the answer should be. The conscious mind, as well as the anti-writer via your preconscious, will have an opinion on the answer and may lead you astray. Let your subconscious answer through your ideomotor responses.

If you wanted to know if you should add a new character to your novel, here is how you would proceed:

> **Question one:** *Subconscious, should I add a new character to my novel?*
> **Answer:** Yes

If your subconscious had said no to this question, you would generate other questions, designed to determine whether to change the setting, the time period, eliminate a character, and so forth.

> **Question two:** *Subconscious, I need to find out the gender of the new character. Is the new character a male?*
> **Answer:** No. (In this case you would then know that the new character is a female.)

You may then want to get an idea of this new female character's age.

> **Question three:** *Subconscious, does this new character need to be younger than age twenty?*
> **Answer:** No

> **Question four:** *Subconscious, does this new character need to be between the ages of twenty-one and forty?*
> **Answer:** Yes

Question five: *Subconscious, is the female character between the ages of twenty-one and thirty?*
Answer: No

Question six: *Subconscious, is the new female character between the ages of thirty-one and thirty-five?*
Answer: Yes

You would continue questioning your subconscious in this manner until you came up with the exact age of your new female character. Depending on your plot, you may have more ideas about how this new female character fits into the story. You could then go on to ask questions related to the plot, the character's appearance, her goals or motivations in the story, her relationship with the hero, heroine, and villain, and so forth. The ways you can use the pendulum to get guidance from your subconscious are virtually endless because your subconscious is giving you guidance on information that it knows and your conscious mind does not. Once you anchor this information in your consciousness, you'll be able to integrate it into your writing.

Handling the Anti-Writer

The anti-writer will attempt to interfere with the information passing from your subconscious into your conscious mind. Let's suppose that your conscious self doesn't want to add a new character even though your subconscious is recommending it. This is why it's important, when using the pendulum process, to be neutral about the information that you are receiving to ensure that your anti-writer is not interfering.

If you get a response that surprises or that doesn't resonate with you, use a bias scale to get clarification from your subconscious about the accuracy of the response. Using a scale from one to ten, with one representing no bias and ten a great bias, ask your subconscious if the bias on the response was greater than five. If you get a positive response to that question, approach the original question from a different angle.

Using the example of adding a new character to your novel, let's say that you are not averse to adding a new character but do not want to add a female, so you ask your question about gender and get a response indicating the character should be male. This doesn't feel right to you, so you re-evaluate using the bias scale. You would ask, "Subconscious, you told me I should add a male but that doesn't seem right. Was the bias greater than five?" If you get a yes response to that question, you will know that your anti-writer is interfering with the flow of information from your subconscious. The more emotion is involved, the more you have to watch out for the anti-writer and do the bias check. The more you practice with the pendulum, the more you will be able to tell when your anti-writer is interfering and mediate its influence.

Using the pendulum is a documented way to communicate with your subconscious mind. For centuries, people have used it to access the subconscious portion of their minds for guidance, inspiration, and solutions to problems. You can do this, too. Making and learning to use a pendulum for subconscious communication is affordable, easy to learn, and can be a significant aid to your creativity.

The Writer's Block

Communicating with your subconscious mind is as easy as using a piece of sewing thread and a washer purchased at any home supply store. This is the pendulum method of subconscious mind communication. It's an easy way to gain access to your subconscious creativity and get your subconscious mind to help you with your writing.

→ Make sure to establish your "code" for subconscious pendulum communication following the instructions in this chapter.

→ The pendulum method of subconscious communication can be used for career guidance, help with plotting and character or scene development, generating ideas for stories, and gaining inspiration for your writing process.

CHAPTER NINE

How *Nature*

Inspires

Creativity

Simply look outside your windows to see a great aid to your writing creativity. The natural world that surrounds you is one of the most powerful stimulants to your creative mind that exists today. Writing has long been associated with nature because the natural world spontaneously stimulates creativity and feelings of well-being, and this leads automatically to the motivation to accomplish goals. Nature offers many benefits to writers, not the least of which is silence and detachment from the hustle and bustle of daily life that cuts you off from your creative core.

Being in nature allows the chatter of the world to die down and your true voice to emerge. It clears a path to your creative mind and allows you to touch that place within yourself where your inspiration resides.

Creative people intuitively take advantage of the creativity that nature can inspire. Albert Einstein was said to have experienced the eureka moment leading to his theory of relativity while taking a walk through the mountains. Classic novelist Carson McCullers would often take long walks in nature, waiting for what she called "the illumination," or the moment that plot points would be revealed to her. Jane Austen immersed herself in the beauty of the meadows surrounding her home, and received many of her ideas while walking there. Novelist Virginia Woolf was known to write with green ink at times in the guesthouse behind her garden, the green ink simulating the green beauty that existed outside of her windows. Even if you live in the inner city and natural areas are sparse, there are easy and affordable ways to capitalize on nature to benefit your writing that will be discussed in this chapter.

The Color of Creativity

The human mind and body have an automatic relaxation response to the color green. This has been primarily documented in medical settings. People in the hospital recover faster when they can see trees outside their window. In one study, two groups of people were exposed to a series of stressful tasks and then one group was allowed to walk along either a nature trail or around a city block. The group that took the nature stroll reported less stress and a quicker return to positive feelings of well-being.

This knowledge can be applied to writing and creativity. Green is linked to relaxation and relaxation is linked to creativity. Capitalizing on the color green to help you relax is an easy way to get into a creative state of mind. The easiest way to benefit from nature and its relaxing effects on the body and mind is to simply immerse yourself in it. Thanks to the National Parks Foundation, which was established in 1967, you can find places in every state in which to hike, camp, or simply spend the day surrounded by the wonders of the natural world. The Foundation's website (*www.nationalparks.org*) has a listing of national parks in all fifty states. Wherever you live, the natural world is nearby, waiting to aid your creativity.

The Voice of Experience

"The color green seems to spark my creativity more than anything. Green rolling pastures, green rainforests, green mountains—they all do the trick."

—Kerrelyn Sparks

All Nature Inspires Creativity

Nature helps you access and free your creativity because the time you spend enjoying it is usually relaxing and unstructured. Many writers use time in and around nature as an opportunity to let their minds free fall, an activity that engages the right brain and allows the subconscious to provide solutions and ideas to the conscious mind. Novelist Judi McCoy lives near a bay where she often seeks refuge after a period of writing. "I like to sit on the sand and stare out and let my mind go," she says. "It's kind of a free fall thing. Generally something falls into place with my writing. I don't censor myself. If I have a neat idea but it doesn't fit with what I'm writing, I go immediately to my idea folder and type it down. I never know when that idea might turn into a book."

Combine your nature walk with your exercise for the day for maximum writing benefit. When you jog, hit the trails of your nearby park to take advantage of the physically relaxing benefits of exertion combined with the color green. Doing this before writing will work off any tension that is blocking your subconscious efforts at creativity.

Use Nature to Relieve Writer's Tension

After a period of intense writing, your brain and body need a break to allow your creative well to refill. This is especially true when you write for a long period of time. Because I work a full-time day job, I typically write for at least four and sometimes as many as eight hours on both Saturday and Sunday to make up for the lost time during the week. I schedule regular walks roughly every two to three hours to let my body loosen up and give my brain a break. I leash my dog and walk on the beach behind my house. The sound of the waves crashing on the shore, watching the pelicans fly overhead, and smelling the salt breeze never fail to undo any tension that has accumulated in my body. When I return to my desk, I feel refreshed and ready to push on for a while longer.

The Voice of Experience

"Writing is a lot like making soup.
My subconscious cooks the idea, but I have to
sit down at the computer to pour it out."

—Robin Wells

A good time to take a break like this is when you come to a natural stopping point in your writing; for instance, when you reach the end of one chapter and before you go on to the next, or after you finish editing the piece and before you start rewriting. Any natural transition period in the work is a good point to do something to refill your well and get the right brain geared up for the next task. Walking in nature is a great way to do this.

Finding Nature

If you have no park, forest, or ocean close by, a walk outside will do the trick. Getting out into the sunshine and fresh air will oxygenate your brain and ease any tension in your hands, arms, and shoulders from writing.

While you walk, scout around your home or apartment for any type of nature that you can walk through or simply stand near for a short time. Even in urban settings, there is usually some type of natural environment nearby that you may have overlooked. When I lived in Atlanta, my house was surrounded in front and back with busy streets and nonstop traffic. It didn't exactly make for a relaxing stroll. But there were two areas where I could access nature in a limited way. The first was a short walking path between two sets of tennis courts that was lined on both sides by pine trees. At the end of the path was a parking lot, but beyond it was a small pond with a fountain. It only took five minutes to walk down the path and through the parking lot to the pond, but just that short interaction with nature usually gave me a boost mentally. I also discovered that the elementary school across the highway had a big playing field that backed up to several acres of heavily wooded private land. I would simply cross that busy street, walk behind the school, and find myself in a quiet, green, tranquil walking retreat. Even though a fence separated me from the woods, I could still see the trees, hear the birds, and bask in the green grass under my feet. Look around your own home and locate natural areas, no matter how small, that can help rejuvenate your creativity on your writing days.

Plant a Garden Outside Your Window

You can use the power of green to stimulate your creativity by planting a garden or trees outside the window in the room where you write. Even if you prefer to write facing a blank wall, which many people do, when you look up or take breaks you can glance outside and see trees, plants, and flowers all of your making. Whenever you take a break from your writing and are either staring out of your window or walking around your neighborhood, focus your attention on the space *between* the trees. Directing your attention to the space between the trees calms the mind, brings your awareness into a small, focused window, and it has the instantaneous effect of reducing tension. This is how novelist Kerrelyn Sparks, who lives in a large city, stays in touch with nature while she's writing. "I only have to look out the window to see a lot of green," she says.

Planting flowers does not have to be elaborate or expensive. Identify a space outside your window for a small garden and purchase plants and flowers of your choosing. Perennials are a good choice to avoid a lot of maintenance since they are usually hardy and you won't have to worry about replanting them. If you are going for green but don't care for color and want little to no maintenance, try planting monkey grass in the area. Plant vegetation that grows to various heights to create an eye catching and soothing view. Day lilies are a good choice for moderately high flowers because they are colorful and hardy.

If you don't have room for a large tree, consider planting a miniature Japanese maple outside your window. Or get a bonsai plant for your desk. These little trees were designed to give the illusion of space, which can create relaxation for the mind and body and open the door to creativity.

Put Plants on Your Desk

If you work outside the home in an office building, you have probably noticed how a plant or two will generate a renewed sense of freshness and calmness to your office space. Just having the color green in your work area will foster the relaxation in your body that will help you gain access to your right-brain creativity.

The Voice of Experience

"The natural environment invigorates me and helps me come up with new ideas for my story."

—Jax Cassidy, author of *The Lotus Blossom Chronicles*

You can do the same thing at your writing desk. Buy plants in whatever size and styles appeal to you and place them around your writing area. Spider plants of all varieties are hardy and require little maintenance, and the long flowing tendrils are pleasant to gaze at. Ferns provide a soft green to hard corners of rooms and the edges of windowsills. African violets are a good choice for window ledges or beside your computer monitor.

I have discovered that even having fake plants in the room is better than nothing. On the days that I write with the blinds closed and the view of my garden obstructed, I find my eye drawn to a fake ivy wreath hanging on the wall near my desk whenever I look up.

Seek Out the Silence in Nature

Silence can be important for some people in order to get into a creative state of mind. Unfortunately, this is hard to do because our world is never silent anymore. Traffic, ringing cell phones, television, computer noise, and the constant immersion in and around other people cuts us off from what Buddhist monks call the "silence beyond the silence," or that inner portion of yourself that is tranquil, at rest, and creative.

Many authors know this intuitively to be true and seek out the silence of nature in any form. Author Molly O'Keefe lives in the city but often takes inspiring walks on the beach to rejuvenate her flagging creativity. The break from the manufactured noise that comes from living in a busy community is eased by the natural sounds of water lapping against the shore. "I live in a city, so I think it's about the silence," she says.

To seek out that deep silence where you can get in touch with your inner creativity, look for a private park bench or find a safe hiking trail and just listen. Sit back and enjoy the silence. Let your mind wander. Don't try to direct it or resolve any problems of any sort. Just allow your mind to drift and meander without any pressure. Focus on your breathing. Many times this type of break from the desk will be the precursor to a breakthrough in creativity. Many creative people report that it is in the brief period of time after they stop working that a solution to a problem occurs to them.

Decorate Your Writing Space

One way you can capitalize on the relaxing qualities of the color green is to use it to decorate your writing space. Simulate the color of nature by choosing emerald greens for drapes, seat covers, cups, and pencil holders. Place green candles around your desk and office space. Paint the walls green or apply wallpaper that has green tones. Any way that you can bring the color green into your writing space will help you create a mind state conducive to creativity and favorable for accessing your subconscious mind.

The Writer's Block

Nature is a powerful aid to the creative process. Nature stimulates creativity and feelings of well-being, which helps create the motivation to accomplish goals. In nature, writers can find many benefits including silence and a sense of detachment from the frenetic pace of daily life. Many writers seek out the solitude and quiet of nature as a way of rejuvenating their creativity. To help nature help you, remember:

- Find a natural area near your home to walk every day; this can be a park, near the beach, or through a wooded area.

- If there are no natural areas where you live, bring nature to you: plant a garden outside your window or bring plants into your writing space.

CHAPTER TEN

Using *Music*

for

Creativity

M usic is a huge part of life and, for writers, it can be an aid for creativity and an inspiration for writing. Authors use music in many ways to inspire and guide their writing sessions, even taking ideas from individual lyrics or writing a scene to the beat of a certain waltz. The use of music has long been a creative aid to many writers, and in this chapter you will learn how you can use this readily available tool to enhance your writing. The ways you can use music for creativity are endless. Certain styles of music, such as baroque, have even been documented to stimulate creativity by helping the brain shift into alpha brain wave mode.

Music as a Creative Tool

Music can be beneficial to the creative state by reducing your perceived level of stress. When you're stressed out, your creativity dries up. It's hard to focus and get into a state of flow with your writing if you're under pressure and keyed up. Listening to music causes positive physiological responses in the body that are characteristic of deep relaxation. Music lowers your blood pressure, breathing rate, heart rate, and skin temperature, which are all physical indicators of stress. Using music to relax before or while you write is an effective way to loosen up your brain and get the words flowing.

The Voice of Experience

"I listen to movie soundtracks because they don't have lyrics and they're emotionally evocative. Music helps guide the meditation process that is involved in tapping into your imagination and the creative process. It puts things in a more cinematic way."

—Zoe Archer, author of *Love in a Bottle* and other novels

When you use music before or during a writing session to aide your creativity, over time you set up what is called in psychology a "conditioned response."

A conditioned response is an acquired response to a previously neutral stimulus. This phenomenon was discovered in the late 1890s by the Russian researcher Ivan Pavlov, who conducted a series of nonharmful experiments with dogs. He paired the ringing of a bell with the presentation of the dog's food and measured their salivation. Initially, the dogs only salivated when they saw and smelled the food. However, over time, Pavlov found that the dogs would salivate when they only heard the bell, meaning that they had come to associate the ringing bell with the presentation of their dinner. The bell became a signal that food was on the way and salivating was a conditioned response to a previously neutral stimulus (the bell).

In terms of writing, this means that you can create a conditioned response in yourself by using music to signal to your subconscious that it's time to get creative. As you begin to write to your chosen music or listen to it prior to writing, over time you will begin to associate hearing that music with writing. With enough repetition, your mind will eventually begin to associate your chosen music with the act of writing. Simply starting the music will become a signal to your subconscious mind that "it's time to write."

The key here is that you are forming an association between your music and writing. This association will grow in strength the more you use it, and this will help you get into a creative zone faster and easier each time you hear the music.

Professional writers have a variety of fun ways to capitalize on establishing a conditioned response between music, creativity, and writing. All of these techniques are easy to use and you can begin implementing them right away to boost your own creative output.

Make a Play List

For each book or writing project that you tackle, identify songs that inspire you to write about the topic or that represent the project's overall message. Collect songs from various artists and put these on your iPod or burn a CD. Then listen to this set of songs *only* when you write on that particular project.

Over time this set of songs will become associated with your writing project and the act of writing it. Each time you listen to that play list, the link between those songs and the writing gets stronger. It builds a bridge from your subconscious to your conscious and helps you access your creative mind faster and easier each time you hear the music.

This is a favorite technique of many professional writers.

The Voice of Experience

"I burn a CD of music that is just for that book. It's like a Pavlovian response. After a while you're into it, and whenever you hear that music you're in that book. I never listen to the CD other than when I'm writing that book."

—Berta Platas

Listening to particular songs repeatedly to help inspire the writing of certain books is a tool that bestselling author Jacquelyn Mitchard uses. "I go through fits of needing to listen to the same song over and over while writing a given book," she says. "For the book *Still Summer* it was 'Claire de Lune.' For the book *The Deep End of the Ocean* it was Puccini's 'Un Bel Di Vedremo.' For *Cage of Stars* it was Emmylou Harris, from 'Red Dirt Girl' to 'If I Needed You.' Right now, it's Audra McDonald singing 'A Sleepin' Bee.'"

The type of music does not matter. It only has to be meaningful to you and your writing project. These songs can represent the theme of your book, evoke the mood of your essay, or remind you of your characters.

Use Music to Write Different Scenes

Different material requires different ways of writing. For example, if you are authoring an action-packed spy novel, writing fast can transfer that feeling of urgency to the scene and add immediacy and tension to the page. In that case, you would want to choose music that has a fast beat and quick tempo. If you're writing a love scene, an emotionally rendered essay designed to generate a lot of feeling in your reader, or a pensive nonfiction article on an important topic, the writing needs to convey leisure, thoughtfulness, and fluidity. In these examples, slower, calmer music can help transfer that tone to your writing.

The Voice of Experience

"I have some CDs which are writing music, and they'll often put me in the zone."

—Jo Beverley

Depending on what type of scene she needs to get down on paper, author Allison Brennan chooses various speeds of music to influence the speed at which she writes. Here's how she does it: for each book, she creates three play lists on her iPod: hard rock, medium rock, and soft rock. She chooses about one hundred songs for each play list. Then, depending on where she is in the novel, she'll play one of those lists while she's writing. "When I'm writing more of the suspense or action I like to listen to hard rock because it's faster," she says. "I find I type faster if the music's faster. If it's a love scene, I tend to go to my soft rock."

Some examples of the hard rock music Brennan listens to while writing her action scenes include:

"Born to Be Wild" by Steppenwolf
"Walk This Way" by Aerosmith
"Shipping Out to Boston" by the Dropkick Murphys

Her medium and soft rock music for love scenes includes:

"(Don't Fear) the Reaper" by Blue Oyster Cult
"I Don't Wanna Be" by Gavin DeGraw
"Paperback Writer" by The Beatles

At the other end of the spectrum is author Cathy Maxwell. She chooses music that helps give an authentic pace to scenes that she's writing. For example, she listens to the actual music that her characters will dance to in a scene in order to transfer the feel of the dance to the characters' movements. "I'll pick a song that they're dancing to and play that repeatedly so that I can get the rhythm of the music into the pattern of the words on the page. For example, if they're waltzing, there's a definite movement involved. I can use the timing of the song to help [write the scene]," she says.

Choose Music to Fit Your Theme

This technique involves identifying a set of songs that represent the theme of your writing project and making a play list according to that theme. For example, author Yasmine Galenorn does this to stay focused on different series' themes when she's writing the next book in the series. She explains that this ensures that each of the stories will have the same tone as the one that went before. An added benefit is that the songs immediately prompt her creative state. "I found a song that fits the mood of my series," she says. "I hear that song and I'm immediately tuned into the series."

Examples of music Galenorn chose for the second book in her urban fantasy series, *Changeling*, include:

"Born on the Bayou" by Creedence Clearwater Revival
"Money for Nothing" by Dire Straits
"The Witch's Promise" by Jethro Tull

Choose Songs with Lyrics That Inspire You

Another way to use songs to inform your writing is to choose music with lyrics that inspire you or inspire a certain idea. This is another technique that Cathy Maxwell uses. In addition to using music to write scenes, she also chooses songs for each book because a phrase in the lyrics catches her attention or captures the message of her story. "Right now I'm working on a book that some of the songs by Coldplay seem to hit the emotions of what it is about," she says. "I've got three Coldplay songs and I'll play them over and over again."

Novelist Molly O'Keefe uses this technique of choosing songs that capture the essence of what she's writing about, but she goes more for the spirit of the song rather than the individual lyrics. Bruce Springsteen is one of her favorite artists to listen to while writing because of the nature of his songs. "He has a handle on heartbreak and hope that I find dovetails nicely with what I try to write," says O'Keefe.

Your own play list with catchy lyrics can be as short as three songs like Maxwell's or as long as one hundred songs like Brennan's. There is no right or wrong way to do this. Simply choose music that is personal and meaningful to you and your writing. The trick to jump-starting your creativity is to listen to this music *only* when you write.

Pick Mood Music

Another fun way to incorporate music into your writing creativity is to pick tunes that match the time period of your writing project. Authors of historical novels do this to make sure they transfer the feel of the setting from the music into their stories. "I have some CDs for my different historical periods to get me into the feel of each," explains author Jo Beverley.

You can do this, too. If you are writing a historical novel, or a piece of nonfiction about a specific time in history, choose music from the particular era of your story's setting. For example, you may choose classical music by Mozart or Vivaldi, or a soundtrack from a movie set in that period. "If I'm doing a Georgian historical, I will sometimes throw baroque on, plus some soundtracks to movies that were set in that time period," says novelist Zoe Archer.

If your story is set in the 1930s or 1940s, play music popular from the time, like Big Band music of Count Basie, Glen Miller, or Duke Ellington. A good movie soundtrack from the 1920s era is *Chicago*. It's easy to find movie soundtracks reminiscent of the 1950s; examples include *Back to the Future Part I*, *Great Balls of Fire*, and *Walk the Line*. The soundtrack from the movie *Starsky and Hutch* is a great choice for music from the 1970s.

The Voice of Experience

"Everyone has their own way to approach a story."

—Lisa Hendrix

You can also pick music that fits the cultural tone of your writing project. For example, if your story is set in another country, find music that is representative of that culture. This is a tool that novelist Zoe Archer uses to bring authenticity to her stories set in other locations. "I just wrote a book set in Mongolia, so I got some Mongolian music with some more adventurous soundtracks," she says.

Mood music is a tool that Danielle Ackley-McPhail, author of *Yesterday's Dreams* and other novels, also uses. She writes novels that are based on Irish mythology, and she chooses music accordingly. "I like to listen to Celtic or folk music, either instrumentals or tracks where the vocals are in a language I don't understand," she says. "I find this kind of music really energizes me and moves me."

Ackley-McPhail adds that she has become so accustomed to the creativity that the music inspires in her that she now listens to this type of music no matter what she's writing.

Listen to Baroque Music

The music of Bach, Vivaldi, Mozart, and other composers who lived between 1600 and the mid-1700s has been found to be emotionally stirring to most people. This style of classical music resonates with most everyone because the rhythm of the music, which is fifty to sixty beats per minute, has soothing physiological effects. Some research indicates that listening to this type of music may improve short-term memory and improve performance on cognitive tasks of short duration. Baroque music has been documented to shift the brain into an alpha wave state; aid relaxation; and heighten a sense of inner awareness and, in turn, creativity. This type of music can be a wonderful aid to relaxation and creativity, either before or during your writing session.

Use Music for Relaxation Before Writing

If listening to music while you write is too distracting, listen to your chosen songs before you write to get inspired and motivated. You can do this while running errands, doing the laundry, or while driving home from work.

Novelist Kerrelyn Sparks finds writing to music too distracting, but she has still found a way to use it in her creativity. "I use music to inspire me," she says. "I usually pick out a theme song for each book, and special songs that represent the hero and heroine. Sometimes I even have music for certain scenes or the black moment—the emotional climax or crisis of a story. I'll listen to these while I'm running errands, and they give me ideas and get me jazzed, so by the time I return home, I'm eager to get back to work."

Author Kristen Painter also listens to music before writing because she prefers silence while working, but she chooses music that matches the mood of the scene she'll be working on later that day. "I listen to music before writing a scene to get me 'in the mood,' be it angry, lonely, happy, or mellow," she says.

Choose music that matches the theme of what you're writing or that has lyrics that inspire you. Before you sit down to write for the day, put on the music and get immersed in the emotion of your story.

Play a Musical Instrument

Playing a musical instrument is a cognitive experience similar to writing, and some research suggests that playing an instrument before you write can help get you into a creative zone. It seems to activate the right brain and jump-start the creative process.

Classic novelist Jane Austen was an accomplished amateur pianist who played the piano every morning before she wrote. Some of the artists she liked to play were Kozeluch, Schubert, and Hoffmeister. Her favorites were sonatas, and she often copied the music onto fresh manuscript paper.

Playing music before writing can act as a warm-up for writing creativity, as demonstrated by novelist Robin Wells. She likes to play the piano before beginning her writing session for the day, and says, "I occasionally play 'The Entertainer' on the piano, and if I play it well, it means my day will go smoothly. There actually seems to be a correlation between how easily I can play the piano on any given day and how easily I can write."

If you already know how to play a musical instrument, you can easily incorporate this technique into your writing day. If you are not proficient in playing an instrument, you can purchase used equipment and start practicing at home. There are online choices for learning to play piano, guitar, and other instruments in the comfort of your own home. You don't have to become an accomplished musician. Just the act of learning to read music and applying this knowledge to an instrument can help bridge your conscious and subconscious minds and aid your creativity.

Using music as a tool to enhance your creativity is an easy and fun way to use a readily available and affordable resource. There are many ways to use this resource to inspire and enhance your writing, from using lyrics as a jumping-off point for character emotions to writing particular scenes to the pace of the music.

The Writer's Block

Music is a common stimulant for creativity used by many writers. It is not uncommon for writers to use music as inspiration for stories, and some take ideas from lyrics or write scenes to certain beats. Baroque music has been documented to stimulate creativity by helping the brain shift into alpha brain wave mode. There are many ways to use music to help you with your writing, including:

- Make a CD of songs that emulate your book's theme and play it only when you write. This sets up a conditioned response that allows you to get back into the story quickly and easily.

- Write to music with either a fast or slow tempo, depending on the pace of your scene.

- Listen to music that inspires you to write before you sit down at your desk.

CHAPTER ELEVEN

Interacting
with Your
Characters

H ave you ever wondered how bestselling authors come up with snappy dialogue or the perfect humorous or dramatic exchange between two characters? Many times they get it by interacting with their characters using a variety of techniques. Interacting with your characters is a way to engage your subconscious processes and stimulate your creativity, especially when your story is stuck. Interviewing and interacting with your characters adds depth to your stories and authenticity to your scenes.

Interacting with your story people is a skill that takes practice, but it can be learned. The nice thing about all of these subconscious communication techniques is that practice makes them easier. As you will see, the process of accessing your subconscious mind becomes more fluid over time so that you can learn to easily slip from writing mode to subconscious communication mode and back to writing mode without ever leaving your desk. Interacting with your characters is a fun way to do that. Interviewing characters is a common way that successful writers pull information from the subconscious into consciousness to benefit their writing and to add realism and complexity to plots.

The Benefits of Interacting with Your Characters

Having a dialogue with characters is something that many writers do as a way to get to know their story people, to add richness to their stories, and to make their plots and characters' lives vivid. This type of exchange lends a sense of reality to the writing that translates to the page. Classic novelist Charles Dickens often interacted mentally with his created characters in order to get to know them. Many contemporary writers do this, too. Author Jo Beverley says this is a great way to get unblocked. "I sometimes do character interviews, writing down the answers," she says. "I find this a great way to get inside a character's head, especially if a book is stalling because I can't figure them out at that time."

The Voice of Experience

"My characters have conversations in my head all the time. It can be disconcerting and distracting, especially when they wake me up at night. Whenever possible I write those down, because that dialogue usually becomes scenes in my books."

—Candace Havens, author of the *Charmed and Dangerous* series

One way to start interacting with your characters is to write down what you hear them say in your head. Often at times when they are not at their computer, many writers have the experience of internally hearing the dialogue between characters. This occurs frequently at night, either through dreams or immediately upon awakening. This is the subconscious mind at work.

Speak the Dialogue

You can interact with your characters by talking out loud to them, or saying aloud the dialogue you are hearing in your head. Interacting with your characters in this way is less structured than interviewing them, which we'll cover next. Speaking the dialogue out loud helps you to clarify points and get deeper into the scene in your mind. Author Molly O'Keefe uses this technique while she's taking relaxing walks on the beach. "When I'm working on a big scene where something big is revealed through dialogue, I am sometimes at the beach with my dog fine-tuning the dialogue out loud," she says. "I want the characters to say the exact right thing that both hammers home the point of the scene or the point of their conflict but that also opens up new conflict. It usually gets pretty heated and I end up spewing it all out loud. Saying it out loud helps me make it concrete so I don't forget."

This can be a great tool to use in overcoming writer's block because engaging in a stream-of-consciousness conversation with your characters stimulates right-brain thinking and helps dislodge logjams in your creative flow. It kicks your creative process into high gear and can often yield fresh and unique ideas for your story. "When I'm stuck, I strike up a mental conversation with my characters to see what their motivations are and where they want to go. For the most part, they tell me exactly what they want," says author Jax Cassidy.

Interacting with the characters often involves slipping into their role in your head, as in this example given by novelist Danielle Ackley-McPhail. "When I am writing a segment and I'm not quite sure where to take it, I actually start to visualize it in my head and slip into the role of whatever character is giving me problems," she says.

Interviewing Your Characters

A good way to get to know your characters and add depth and scope to your story people is to interview them. This is a structured and methodical process whereby you inquire about their occupations, their avocations, their family structure, their likes and dislikes, their childhood, and so on. Anything is fair game for an interview. Ask about how they are feeling that day, what they did last night for fun, why they are dressed the way they are today. Maybe they're smoking a cigarette and you previously did not know that they smoked. Character interviews are only limited by your imagination.

Interviewing characters is an excellent way to glean new directions for your plot, gain a more in-depth understanding of your characters' motivations, and figure out what direction your story needs to go. Any time you find yourself needing more information about your story, your characters, or what happens next, simply ask your story people. Speak directly to them. You can increase your focus by closing your eyes and picturing your character's face in front of you. Ask direct questions about what happens next in the plot, what secrets your characters hold, why your heroine is thrilled to learn that her new next-door neighbor is her ex-husband, and so forth. Do not censor the responses. Allow your subconscious mind to provide you with the answers. Write them down as they occur to you.

Open-Ended Questions

There are certain techniques for interviewing people that are designed to elicit information. All of these techniques use *open-ended* questions. Open-ended questions are those to which a simple yes or no response cannot be given. For instance, "Do you like coffee?" is a *closed-ended* question because the person can give a yes or no response without any further elaboration. You do not get any new details or insights about a person using close-ended questions.

Open-ended questions encourage elaboration and help stimulate the creative process. For example, "What did you enjoy most about your vacation?" is an example of an open-ended question. You can see how these questions are phrased in such a way that gives the person an opportunity to provide new information and details about themselves, as well as reveal feelings. A good open-ended question allows a person to discover insights that they may not even be aware of yet. For example, if one of your characters is acting sullen during your interview and in the last chapter you know he had a fight with his girlfriend, you might want to explore his current feelings to determine how he will act next. Is he totally fed up with his girlfriend and in the process of looking for another place to live? Does he feel guilty because he thinks the fight is his fault and he's afraid she'll leave him now? Or is he indifferent, believing that the fight yesterday won't make a whit of difference in their relationship? How he feels will determine your writing for the day. To get to his feelings and encourage him to elaborate, you might ask something such as, "You seemed pretty angry when you left the house. How do you think the argument will impact your relationship?" The character could then confirm he's angry or correct you by supplying the way he really feels. Let's say he replies, "I am angry, but at myself, not her."

Then he's just revealed a new element to the story. Why would he be angry with himself about the fight? Ask him using an open-ended question to continue to probe the character's feelings.

Paraphrasing

Paraphrasing is a good technique to use along with open-ended questions to dig deeper into a person's emotions. It can add depth to your story, especially when a character is acting in unexpected ways or you need to flesh out a certain emotion. Paraphrasing is simply making an observation about what you have seen or heard the person do or say in order to seek clarification and gain deeper understanding. Continuing with our example above, you can paraphrase the situation by saying, "That was a bad fight you two had in the last scene. I would imagine you are feeling very angry right now."

Summarizing allows your character to clarify his true feelings—he might come back at you and say, "No, I wasn't angry. I didn't mean to slam the door so hard."

Or he might say, "You're right; I'm angry and I'm going to stay angry until she apologizes."

With either response, you are gathering more insight into the character's motivations and can write the next scenes with more validity.

Any question that begins with "Tell me about . . ." or "What are your thoughts on . . ." or "How do you feel about . . ." are good open-ended questions because they leave the response field wide open. You are not leading the person to a specific answer, you are giving the character room to generate an individual response without undue influence from you.

Coffee with Your Characters

Having coffee with your characters is a concept presented in a recurring post on the Motivated Writers Life Blog (*www.themotivatedwriter.com*), created by Su Kopil. The idea behind the activity is that while you are drinking your first cup of coffee of the day (or tea or juice), you start to communicate with your subconscious mind by pretending you are sitting across from the character you intend to write about that day. Imagine that they are joining you in your morning beverage. Engage in an imaginary conversation with them to jump-start your right-brain, creative mind.

Taken with permission from a sample post on the Motivated Writers Life Blog, some of the questions you could ask while having coffee with your character include:

- What secrets does he share?
- What does she complain about?
- What is he wearing today? Has he shaved or is he going with the rumpled look and why?

If you are working with your antagonist or villain, pretend you are sitting in a coffee shop and your character walks in:

- How does he treat other customers?
- How is she dressed?
- What does he order?
- Is she carrying a newspaper, glancing furtively over her shoulder?

Interacting with your characters via interviews, paraphrasing, slipping into their role in the story, or having coffee with them are all good ways to tap into subconscious creativity and add depth to your writing. Interviewing characters is a fun and easy way to warm up to your writing and get back into the flow of your story. It also allows you to really get to know your characters, which will add realism and richness to your work.

Accessing your subconscious mind and its infinite resources for creativity is the first step in freeing your creative mind. We will now move into the second set of techniques: tools for programming your subconscious mind.

The Writer's Block

Interacting with your characters is a fun and easy way to stimulate the subconscious creative process while writing. It's a common way that successful writers tap into their subconscious mind for writing benefit and get to know their characters on a deeper, more complex level. Remember:

- •→ Interacting with characters allows you to learn about their motivations.

- •→ Interviewing characters helps writers get to know their story people.

- •→ Writers often interact with their characters as a way of developing their plots and creating scenes.

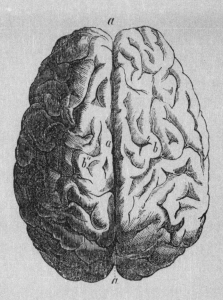

part iii

Programming Your Subconscious Mind

CHAPTER TWELVE

Your *Personal*

Writer's

Gold Mine

Your subconscious mind is your most powerful tool as a writer; it's like your own personal gold mine of creative material. Tapping
into your personal writer's gold mine is as simple
as accessing the enormous power of your subconscious mind and programming it for maximum creative gain. The techniques you learned
in Part I were tools for gaining access to the
creative material in your subconscious, and now
that you've learned how to use these techniques,
you need to learn to program your subconscious
mind for maximum creativity.

Programming your subconscious mind consists of using a
simple formula for influencing your subconscious to create
certain realities for you as a writer, whether it's to achieve

your lifelong writing goals, land your ideal agent, or get your name on the *New York Times* bestseller list. This formula is: genuine intention + repetition + burning desire = subconscious programming. The elements of this formula *influence* your subconscious mind to bring about the outcomes of your programming in various ways that we will discuss in this section. All of the techniques in this section of the book use this formula to help you program your subconscious mind for maximum creativity and to help you reach your writing goals quickly and easily.

Subconscious Programming = Genuine Intention + Repetition + Burning Desire

First let's take a look at the formula for harnessing the power of your subconscious mind and influencing it to help you make certain conditions a reality. For our purposes, influencing the subconscious mind means programming it to help you meet your short- and long-term writing goals, whatever they may be.

As mentioned previously, many authors and motivational speakers have discussed the concept of the subconscious mind creating your reality, beginning with Napoleon Hill's 1937 classic self-help book *Think and Grow Rich*. But one thing that is often overlooked is how, exactly, do you use your subconscious mind to create that reality? The answer is that you have to learn to influence your subconscious mind to do certain things by programming it; a critical step in manifesting your writing goals. Again, you program your subconscious mind through the combination of genuine intention, repetition, and burning desire. Let's look at each of these three required elements separately.

Genuine Intention

Genuine intention is the first step in the programming formula. To make something happen, you have to convince the subconscious mind that you really want it to happen. Half-hearted approaches do not send a message to the subconscious of genuine intentions to succeed. If your subconscious mind responded to every insincere or off-the-cuff thought you had, the results could be disastrous. For example, most everyone has been through a low period in life and had the thought, "I wish I were dead."

Clearly, most people don't really want to be dead when they have thoughts like that; they're just feeling temporarily distressed. The subconscious does not act on such a thought because the conscious mind is not genuine in its intent.

Taking baby steps is a good way to increase your conscious intent to succeed. Basically, you break your large goals down into smaller goals that you know you can easily reach. For example, the goal "I will write a novel" can be overwhelming, and feeling overwhelmed can lead you to doubt your ability to accomplish the goal. To increase genuine intent in your conscious mind, turn this goal into "I will write one page per day."

As you begin reaching this smaller goal, it convinces your conscious mind that you can achieve the goal, and so you raise the bar. The next step is "I will write three pages a day."

When you reach that goal easily, you again push the bar higher until you are convinced that you can reach your overall goal of writing a novel.

Lack of genuine intent is usually caused by lack of belief in your ability to reach the goals you have set for yourself as an aspiring writer. Let's say you have as a goal to become a *New York Times* bestselling author. There's nothing wrong with that. Setting big goals gives you the motivation to keep going, keeps you on track with your plans, and gives your daily efforts a sense of purpose and meaning. All of those things are important in the life of a writer.

When talking about goals, a staircase analogy is useful. So in this example the big goal—to become a *New York Times* bestselling author—is at the top of your stairs. As an aspiring writer standing at the bottom looking up, it can be difficult for you to really believe you can reach that goal. Doubt whittles away your genuine intent, and the subconscious mind—which constantly monitors and records everything going on inside of you—picks up on that. So you may tell yourself a thousand times an hour that you are a *New York Times* bestselling author, but if there is any doubt whatsoever in your conscious mind, the subconscious mind will ignore your attempts at programming and will not process the information needed to make the dream a reality. Genuine intent is critical to influencing your subconscious mind, and to get genuine intent you first need genuine belief.

The trick to gaining genuine belief is to focus on the baby steps, or the in-between steps, that lead to the top of the staircase. Again, start with a goal you know you can reach and work your way up from there. Shift your focus from the top of the staircase to the middle. Maybe finishing your novel in a year is the goal at the middle of the staircase. That's something you believe you really can do since you know you can write one page per day. Genuine belief creates genuine intent, which in turn influences your subconscious mind to yield its help to your programming efforts.

Maybe your next interim goal is to land an agent. Take baby steps to reach that goal, such as polishing your manuscript, researching agents, putting together a compelling synopsis, and so on. When you get an agent, your confidence grows again. You take another step up your staircase. Then the next interim goal is to get a major house to publish your book. And so on. In this way, you climb your staircase one step at a time, with your subconscious behind you all the way.

This is a subjective activity. Only you can know how convinced you are of reaching certain goals. Whenever you are unsure, start out with goals that you know that you can reach with ease and then increase the difficulty of your goals slowly over time. In this way, you will increase your conscious mind's genuine intent to succeed and begin the programming process of your subconscious.

Repetition

The second key element for subconscious programming is repetition. In order to program your subconscious mind, you must repeat your intent consistently over a period of time. You can have conscious intentions all day long, but if you do not repeatedly express what you intend to have happen, your subconscious will not be influenced to any great degree and the programming formula will not work. In other words, just saying one time, "I will write one page per day" will not have an effect on your subconscious because you have only expressed the intention once. To influence your subconscious, it's something that you need to repeat to yourself over and over during the day. If you want to write one page per day, frequently imagine yourself writing that one page. Simply think about it as often as you can. This repetitive thinking helps generate conscious intent. Repetition, or constant mental immersion in the outcome, is necessary for subconscious programming. The subconscious mind is highly susceptible to suggestion because it is neutral. It does not assign a good or bad value to any information it receives from the conscious mind; it simply accepts whatever it is told if it is told often enough.

This is where your Vision of Success—a mental photograph of what writing success means to you—can help. It's the final outcome of what you're striving toward. It could be working as a freelance writer for national magazines, landing a particular agent, making the *New York Times* bestseller list, or becoming an award-winning poet. Whatever writing success means to you, right down to the smallest detail, is what makes up your Vision of Success. When you have a single image of this success that you can hold in your mind all the time, you are putting into action the element of repetition for subconscious influence and programming.

Burning Desire

The final element required for subconscious programming is burning desire. Desire is different from intent. Intent is at the thinking level: "I am determined to finish my novel." Desire is at the feeling level: "When I finish my novel, I'll feel great about myself because I'll be fulfilling a lifetime dream." Desire is the fuel that charges the conscious intent and the catalyst that stimulates conscious repetition. When you really want something, you think about it all the time.

Desire is a powerful motivator. It makes your conscious intent genuine and forces repetitive thinking, which in turn influences your subconscious mind to begin processing information that will make that intention a reality. This kind of desire is what can be called the Burning Desire to Write—that continual, nagging urge to write that can only be satisfied by writing. It's the classic sign that you are a writer.

These three elements combined convince the subconscious mind that you are serious about meeting your writing goals. This formula is the key to using your subconscious mind to create a particular reality.

Positive Declarations and Imagery

To use this formula of subconscious programming for maximum effect, you can use a technique that I call positive declarations and imagery (PDI). The PDI method influences your subconscious to bring both your short-term writing goals and your long-term aspirations into reality through the repetitious act of declaring—via words and images—your various goals in a scheduled and methodical way. When using PDI to reach your goals, the key to success is to use your programming formula: verbalize your statement (repetition), visualize the end result (genuine intent), and then take the action (burning desire). Essentially, you feed your subconscious mind a series of statements and pictures that represent what you are striving to achieve.

A Positive Self-Fulfilling Prophecy

Using positive declarations and imagery is a system known in psychology as a *self-fulfilling prophecy*—something that you tell yourself over and over that eventually becomes true. In other words, you convince yourself of something over time and then act in ways that bring about that particular circumstance.

Let's say that one of your problems is that you write too slowly. You have been telling yourself repeatedly for many years, "I write slowly." Eventually, because you have verbalized that statement so often and imagined yourself writing slowly so frequently, the situation becomes a reality even if it wasn't the case initially. The repetition created intent and desire in the conscious mind to write slowly, which in turn influenced the subconscious mind to make that situation a reality.

Situations like this exist in every aspect of writing. Many years ago I balked at the idea of rising at 3:30 A.M. to write before I left for my day job. I told myself that I couldn't do it. I imagined myself struggling to wake up before dawn, groggy and muddled. Compounding the issue was that ever since childhood, my family had been telling me that I wasn't a morning person. It had always been hard for my mother to get me up for school, and

I'm very quiet and withdrawn during the first part of the day. Because of this, I believed that I was not capable of getting up early, much less writing during that time. Because I believed it, I repeated the statement often to myself and others and this created the self-fulfilling prophecy of a person who was not capable of getting up early to write.

That changed when I realized that early morning was the only time I had available to pursue my dreams of writing. So to turn things around, I began telling myself that I was an early riser. I stated out loud that I got up at 3:30 every morning to write. I visualized myself doing so each night when I set the alarm clock. Because the conscious mind can only hold one thought at a time, I held the picture of me getting up and going to my desk to write firmly in my consciousness.

The Voice of Experience

"People are drawn to being writers because they already have that native inspiration within them."

—Zoe Archer

Next, I took action. I began forcing myself to get up when the alarm went off, all the while telling myself I was a morning person and holding in mind the image of me writing in the morning. After a few months, the programming took hold and it became easy for me to get up early to write. Now, after years of programming and taking the action that reinforced that programming, sticking to my early morning writing routine is effortless. The biggest surprise was that, contrary to what I'd been taught to believe about myself, the mornings turned out to be my most creative period of the day. That's the *real* reason I was always quiet and withdrawn at the breakfast table.

Let's go back to the example of believing that you write too slowly. To correct this and set up a new self-fulfilling prophecy, you would need to start saying, "I write fast," and visualize yourself writing fast. You would then need to follow up these positive declarations and imagery with action to reinforce the PDI. When you sit down to write, intentionally write faster than you normally do. Over time, the conscious mind's intention shifts and the subconscious mind is influenced to bring about a different outcome.

You can apply this principle to any area of your writing life. If you constantly make the statement that you are a creative, disciplined person and imagine yourself doing things that a creative disciplined person would do, you will begin acting as if you have those traits and—through genuine intention, repetition, and burning desire—your subconscious will eventually bring that state into being.

Consistency Is Key

The key to using PDI to create a positive self-fulfilling prophecy is *consistency*. You must always talk and think about yourself in positive terms, including in conversations with other people. Using the example of the slow writer, you must never allow yourself to characterize your writing as slow when talking to people in your critique group or at a writing conference, for example. If you are telling yourself "I am a fast writer" but say to your peers, "I write too slowly," you've just neutralized your PDI and reinforced the wrong thing—that you're a slow writer. So when creating a self-fulfilling prophecy, be consistent at all times with the messages you are sending your subconscious. Remember that the conscious mind can only hold one thought at a time; make sure yours is positive.

Programming Statements

Another fast and easy way to positively program your subconscious mind is to use one-line, declarative statements. These statements are phrased in the present tense. For maximum impact, you state, "I am a bestselling author" rather than "I will be a bestselling author." Because the second statement is presented as an event in the future, your subconscious mind will constantly push it to the future and it will not become a reality. PDI statements phrased in the present tense create genuine intention and desire in the conscious mind.

Positive programming statements should also be phrased in affirmative rather than negative terms. For example, rather than saying, "I will not oversleep and miss my writing time," you would say "I wake up early and get my writing completed." The second statement is stronger and your subconscious mind takes it as an actual event since you are stating it in the present tense.

Successful writers use positive programming statements to help them in their day-to-day writing. "I sometimes write, 'I write easily and well' over and over," says novelist Robin Wells. "It makes me feel as if I'm doing something positive to empower my writing."

The Voice of Experience

"I have been known to say, audibly,
'Jackie, you can do this. . . .'"

—Jacquelyn Mitchard

Positive programming is a good way to stay on track with your short-term writing goals and inspire you to take action toward reaching them. It's a tool that has worked for novelist Bonnie Edwards. She says that after defining her idea of success and understanding that wishes are not the same as goals, she wrote up a positive programming statement and stuck it on her computer monitor. It states: *I am a multipublished author working with an editor who loves my work.*

If you have had trouble reaching a particular goal, examine the possibility that it's because genuine intent does not exist in your conscious mind due to self-doubt. If you feel that that is the case, lower your sights on your staircase—what is an in-between, interim goal that you know you can reach? Turn the goal into a positive programming statement.

Below are examples of positive programming statements related to writing. Use these or create your own based on your own goals.

- I write easily and well every day.
- I am creative.
- I write fast.
- I am writing a book.
- Ideas come to me easily.
- Writing is easy for me.
- I complete my writing goals every day.
- I always have plenty of motivation to write.
- I am in touch with an endless stream of creativity.
- I remember my dreams vividly.
- Ideas come to me through my dreams.
- I always have time to write.
- I meet my word count every day.
- I am a published author.

Creative Visualization

Creative visualization is a form of PDI that you may already be familiar with. Similar to daydreaming, creative visualization allows you to methodically influence your subconscious mind. There are several ways that you can use creative visualization to achieve writing success.

To Achieve Your Vision of Success

Successful writers know what they want and they daydream about it all the time. They use their creative imagination not only to pen fiction and nonfiction but to create their own life and success. They visualize all aspects of a writing career, including landing their ideal agent or publisher.

Author Molly O'Keefe daydreamed constantly about getting a phone call from her agent that a publisher was willing to pay for her book, and it eventually happened. She says imagining success was critical to keeping her motivation high, especially in the early days of rejection. "The only way to stay sane in this game and to keep putting your butt in the chair despite the writer's block, the rejection, the constant doubt and worry is to imagine that you've succeeded," she says. "And the more you imagine, the longer you stay in the chair, the harder you work, the closer you get to making it happen. That's what I believe. And yes, it worked incredibly."

Daydream about your Vision of Success to generate genuine intention in your conscious mind and program your subconscious to make it a reality.

To Achieve Short-Term Goals

There is no limit to the ways you can use creative visualization to help you achieve your writing goals. Let's say you want to write a query letter this weekend. During the preceding week, write down all of the steps necessary to complete this goal, and then spend time every day imagining yourself doing those steps. This might include sitting down at your desk, conducting research, drafting the letter, printing it out, editing it, placing it in the addressed envelope, and mailing it. Whatever steps are necessary for you to complete the goal of writing a query letter should be visualized ahead of time to create genuine intention in your conscious mind, which in turn programs your subconscious mind to make it happen.

To Visualize Words Flowing

This technique is one of my favorites because it helps get me through any dry spells in my writing. Whenever you get stuck, simply imagine the words in your head flowing down your arms, through your hands, and into the keyboard. Sit for a few minutes in silence and *see* the words flowing like water out of your brain and into your computer or notebook. This is a great exercise to use any time you get stuck or want to write fast.

The Voice of Experience

"I say, 'I'm going to write a book,' and I've opened the portal in my mind to possibility thinking."

—Cathy Maxwell

Send a Bouquet

Visualize sending a bouquet of flowers before you conduct a pitch session with an editor or agent. In your mind, imagine yourself smiling and extending a fragrant bunch of flowers to the person you are going to be pitching your manuscript to; this imagery can create positive energy between you and the other person ahead of time, and it can also change the energy from negative to positive if things aren't going well during the pitch.

Bedtime Visualization

A good time to do creative visualization is right before going to sleep. This way, you take advantage of the hypnagogic state and give a direct visual command to your subconscious about what you want.

Novelist Judi McCoy employed this technique with great success. "Every night before I went to sleep, I saw in my mind my name on the spine of a book, in the book store, next to Judith McNaught," she says. "I didn't know what the title was, it had no color; it was just my name on the spine on a bookshelf. I envisioned that in my brain and told myself that was going to be me. I was going to have that book on the shelf in a bookstore. It was going to happen. That was my mantra every night going to bed." The result of McCoy's nightly use of bedtime visualization was having her books in the bookstore, just as she had imagined.

You can also use visualization to imagine your end goal. If you want to finish your novel, visualize the book as done and complete. This is a technique that author Lori Devoti employs. "I *see* the book finished," she says. "I just see me being done with it, meaning hitting 'the end.'"

PDI is one of the most powerful tools you have for accomplishing your writing goals. On the CD that accompanies this book, you will find an exercise that will assist you in learning how to use imagery for writing success. The track contains a visualization designed to help you make a successful pitch to an agent at a conference. Once you learn the technique, you can then substitute any writing-related goal into the visualization exercise.

A Real-Life Example of Subconscious Programming

Programming the subconscious mind using genuine intent, repetition, and burning desire is the secret to influencing your subconscious to bring about desired results. Novelist Robin Wells uses this formula to accomplish certain goals related to her writing career. Notice how her statement contains all of the necessary elements of subconscious influencing: "Once I started writing, there was no turning back. I *had* to get published. *[Genuine intent.]* I *was going to* get published. I *knew* I would get published. I believed, down in the depths of my soul, that if I did the work, I would get the result. *[Repetition.]* It might take a long time, but I would get there. I had an obsessive sort of iron-clad determination." *[Desire.]* Wells's mindset contained all three required elements of subconscious programming, and it worked. She has now published thirteen books.

Programming your subconscious mind is a powerful way to achieve all of your writing goals, and the formula is simple to use. Create genuine intent in your conscious mind by setting goals you know you can reach, repeat the goal over time to influence your subconscious, and generate burning desire by imagining your accomplishment and the good feelings that will go along with achieving it.

The Writer's Block

Bring your goals into reality by programming the subconscious mind. For maximum effect, use this simple formula: subconscious programming = genuine intent + repetition + burning desire. Combined, these three elements help you influence your subconscious mind to bring about the results you want in your writing life. Positive Declarations and Imagery (PDI)—positive programming statements combined with various forms of visualization—create a mental picture that provides fuel to your powerful subconscious mind. Remember:

- If you are having trouble generating genuine intent to reach a goal, start with baby steps, those small goals that you know you can accomplish.

- Positive Programming statements are always stated in the present tense.

- Bedtime is a good time to use Positive Programming because you can capitalize on the hypnagogic state.

CHAPTER THIRTEEN

The *Power*

of Suggestion

and Belief

W hat do you tell yourself about you as a writer? Suggestion is a powerful tool for freeing your creative mind, one that can make or break you when it comes to meeting your short- and long-term writing goals. Suggestion and belief are related because, over time, suggestions form your beliefs, and beliefs in turn reinforce the suggestions you give yourself about writing and creativity.

Because it is neutral, the subconscious mind is highly susceptible to suggestion, receiving information from the conscious mind without assigning a value, and simply accepting whatever it is told. Therefore—in addition to the positive programming statements and creative visualizations that you learned in the last chapter—you can use the powerful tool of suggestion to aid your creative process and lay a foundation for maximizing your creative output.

141

How Suggestion and Belief Work Together

Suggestion is a pervasive form of self-programming. Because it occurs continually, you need to take control of it to weed out the negative and focus on the positive—or create it if need be. Suggestion is the foundation of your beliefs about yourself as a writer and, over time, establishes how you view yourself and your creativity. Suggestion can be very subtle and yet with repetition, it can be very powerful, too.

Suggestion forms beliefs by pairing an emotional response to a previously neutral thought. For example, if you are bombarded by suggestions from yourself and others that you are creative and talented, you will begin acting talented and creative even if you don't initially feel that way. As you begin to act like a talented and creative person, you begin to feel that way, forming the belief that you are talented and creative. You will begin to spend time with your writing, and when you sit down at your desk your creativity will flourish. The suggestion will manifest itself as an outburst of creative writing, and the belief will solidify.

The Voice of Experience

"I try to keep my energy on my writing and my choices. I think it's about being positive."

—Molly O'Keefe

The opposite is also true. If you send yourself messages or suggestions that you are not talented and creative, over time you begin to believe and act as if you are not. This will show itself by how you manage your time. You won't make the time to write or, if you do, you will sit and stare at the blank paper. Words won't flow. You will repeatedly tell yourself that you aren't creative and, because this suggestion will take root in your subconscious, you will begin to believe this over time and it will become your reality.

There are many ways that you can use the power of suggestion to free your creative mind and talents and increase your writing output. Some are discussed below.

The Most Powerful Suggestion: Action

Your behavior and actions are a powerful subconscious suggestion because how you conduct yourself on a daily basis impresses upon your subconscious mind what you believe about yourself. Remember how I didn't believe I could get up early to write because I thought I was not a morning person? However, when I took action in the opposite direction and started rising at 3:30 A.M., my actions neutralized the previous suggestions and became a new, more powerful influence on my subconscious mind that allowed me to act in a different way than I had formerly believed I could. So if you believe you're a writer, you will write. More importantly, when you write you are convincing your conscious mind that you are a writer and cultivating genuine intent. The action itself is the suggestion.

In many twelve-step self-help groups there is a saying: Take the action and the feeling will follow. This means that you have to act your way into feeling, not the other way around. In other words, if you want to feel creative, act creative first. If you want to feel like a writer, act like a writer first. Your own behavior is the most powerful suggestion you can give to your subconscious mind. If you want to form the belief that you are a creative, talented writer, act your way there.

Make a Commitment to Your Writing

Making a commitment to writing is a powerful way to suggest to your subconscious mind that you are a creative, talented writer. Step up and say, out loud, "I am a writer." Look at yourself in the mirror when you say it. Write it down as one of your positive programming statements.

An incredible thing happens when you make a commitment to writing: you start writing. If you were writing inconsistently before, suddenly you find yourself looking for time during the day to write. You get more ideas. Obstacles that once prevented you from writing suddenly seem easy to overcome. You decide that nothing will stop you from reaching your writing goals, whatever they may be. Finding that internal footing is a powerful suggestion to your subconscious mind that strengthens over time.

Novelist Allison Brennan experienced the power of commitment before she became a successful, published author. Brennan started but never finished more than one hundred books until she finally made the commitment to see one through. It made all the difference in the world for her career. "My turning point was when I made the commitment," she says. "For me it was like flipping an internal switch. I convinced myself that if I was ever going to be published, I had to finish something."

This commitment to writing suggested to Brennan's subconscious mind that she was going to make it as a writer, and her behavior reflected this belief. Before receiving a scathing rejection for the first manuscript she submitted, Brennan demonstrated her commitment to writing by finishing a second novel. The commitment to writing saw her through the rejection of the first book and helped pave her way to success. "I could see that my writing got better with each book," she says. "And if each book is better, then at some point it would be good enough to get published. It might take ten books, I didn't know. I was willing to keep writing them."

Give your subconscious mind the suggestion that you are a creative, talented writer by making a commitment to writing. Say it out loud: "I am committed to writing." Or, "I make a commitment to get in touch with my subconscious creativity." Write it down on an index card and hang it where you will see it constantly; in the bathroom, on the refrigerator, or next to your computer. The more you can impress this suggestion upon your subconscious mind, the faster and easier it will be for you to start acting like a committed writer and begin seeing results.

The Voice of Experience

"If I'm having plot problems, I say, 'You are a talented writer, you have worked this out before and you'll work it out again.'"

—Susan Elizabeth Phillips

Support Forms Positive Suggestions and Beliefs

Another good way to give your subconscious mind the constant suggestion that you are a writer and have maximum creative output is to surround yourself with people who reinforce this. You can do this by joining writers' associations, a local chapter of your writing genre's group, or by forming a group on your own with other aspiring writers to offer mutual help and support on a regular basis.

Bestselling authors use the support of other writers as a tool to keep those positive suggestions about their writing and creativity flowing in. "My biggest creative recharging comes from talking to other writers, brainstorming over lunch or coffee," says author Barbara Freethy. "I find that even brainstorming another writer's plot helps me to get into the creative mode and gets me excited to work on my own story."

Having a support group of other aspiring writers is a good way to provide constant stimulation to your creativity, and has the added benefit of helping you get through any periods of feeling stuck in your writing. This is a key reason that Monica McCarty, *New York Times* and *USA Today* bestselling author of *Highlander Unchained* and other novels, has a support group of writers. "I do have times where I am blocked," she says. "Usually what I do is talk it out with a friend. Just phrasing the problem opens it up, and talking through the issue helps you see a couple of different answers and pick which one you want to do."

When forming a positive-suggestion support group, look for people who have writing goals similar to yours and who are actually writing, not just talking about writing. Ensure that the suggestions these people give you will be positive and helpful. That's not to say that you should never be given feedback that helps you improve as a writer, because that is part of why you want a critique group—to get better. But there's a way to deliver feedback to help someone improve. An aspiring writer recently told me that someone in her critique group said that an early draft of her novel was the worst example of first-person point of view that he had ever seen. That kind of negativity is not helpful and can be extremely discouraging, especially for new writers. Avoid people who will give you harsh criticism and, instead, surround yourself with those who will couch their feedback in a more supportive manner.

Record Suggestions

Remember the hypnagogic state from Chapter 6? That is a fertile time to program your subconscious mind to realize that you are a creative, talented, successful writer. Write out your positive suggestions related to your writing goals, then purchase a small digital recorder and read your suggestions into the recorder. Turn it on at night when you go to sleep and let the suggestions slip directly into your subconscious. The digital recorder will shut itself off when it's finished, so you can simply go to sleep and allow your mind to be programmed for creativity.

Write "I" Sentences

Remember when you were a kid and you had to write sentences as punishment? It was usually something like "I will not run in the hall" or "I will not talk back to the teacher," and you had to write them ten times on the board or one hundred times in your notebook over the weekend. These sentences were designed to change your behavior for the better; the problem is that because they were phrased in the negative, all they did was make you think about the very behavior the teacher was trying to eliminate, thereby actually increasing the chances that the behavior would occur again.

If you want to become a writer, you need to focus on the steps you should take to get there. Motivational author Brian Tracy recommends defining the steps you need to take to meet your long- and short-term writing goals, and then writing those steps ten times in a notebook at least once a day. Two times a day is better, perhaps when you get up in the morning and before you go to bed at night. This is an excellent way to make suggestions to your subconscious mind.

Perhaps you want to plan the steps necessary to finish one chapter of your novel each month. First, outline the necessary steps; your plan may be as straightforward as: "I will write three pages in the evening when I get home from work, every Monday through Friday." Write that statement in your notebook ten times each morning and night as a way to suggest to your subconscious mind to follow through on that plan.

You can break down the plan further by writing out the steps that lead up to writing three pages each evening. This is especially good to do if you need to identify stumbling blocks in meeting your short-term goal. Let's say you intend to write for thirty minutes before the family arrives home in the evening, but are consistently delayed by preparing dinner and last-minute household chores. Your steps might look something like this: I set the egg timer for thirty minutes as soon as I get home, I put dinner in the oven, I take the phone off the hook, I feed the cat, I sit down at my desk and write three pages. Notice that those statements are written as "I" sentences in order to make them more powerful to your subconscious. Using "I" statements sends a potent suggestion to your subconscious mind that greatly influences your behavior.

Write down your "I" steps every day until the desired behavior is reached. Once the habit of the behavior is formed, you can switch to different statements if you wish or, if you find yourself slacking off from writing three pages each day, start up with the "I" sentences again. Be sure to identify the obstacles to your writing, because you want to address them in your sentences.

Remember that the suggestions you give your subconscious should always be positive and uplifting, because suggestion and belief go hand-in-hand when it comes to accessing your subconscious mind and freeing your creativity. Using the techniques in this chapter, you can intentionally feed your subconscious mind suggestions that will form powerful and influential beliefs in your subconscious and help you achieve your writing goals quickly and easily.

The Writer's Block

Your neutral subconscious mind is highly susceptible to suggestion. It receives information from the conscious mind, without assigning it a good or bad value; it simply accepts whatever it is told. Suggestion is a powerful aid to your creative process, therefore, you can feed your subconscious mind positive images that help you reach your writing goals. Remember:

➥ Suggestion and belief work together to influence the subconscious mind. Whatever you suggest to your subconscious mind, over time, also becomes your belief.

➥ The most powerful suggestion to your subconscious mind is the action you take toward meeting your writing goals, because feeling follows action.

CHAPTER FOURTEEN

Mental Rehearsal

Mentally practicing something that you want to perform well is a tried and true technique that athletes have been using for decades to improve their athletic abilities. The principles of mental rehearsal apply to writing, too, and you can learn to capitalize on this tool to enhance your creativity and meet your writing goals.

For the purposes of writing, mental rehearsal is a deepening of the practice of PDI and creative visualization to enhance your performance in any given area of writing or to aid you in reaching a certain goal. It's the practice of performing an activity in your mind before you actually do it in order to increase your chances of getting the results that you want, and it can be used to meet both long- and short-term writing goals.

How Mental Rehearsal Works

Mental rehearsal is similar to using PDI to reach your writing goals except that you expand on and deepen the imagery to include critical steps necessary to reach your goal. Mental rehearsal is different from creative visualization alone. With creative visualization you are working to achieve your Vision of Success, but with mental rehearsal, you mentally practice the behaviors that will lead to the attainment of your goals. It is another way to use genuine intention + repetition + burning desire to influence your subconscious mind to produce results.

A fascinating aspect of mental rehearsal is that it not only affects your subconscious mind, it affects your body too. When you mentally practice a certain behavior, such as sitting down at your desk and writing for a certain amount of time every day, you gradually create physiological changes in your body that will support this behavior. Researchers have found evidence to support this phenomenon. Studies using an EMG, a machine that measures how brain impulses affect neuromuscular activity, have demonstrated that mentally rehearsing an activity causes the same neurons to fire within the body exactly as if the person were actually physically carrying out the task. This means that you can program both your mind *and* your body to support your writing endeavors using mental rehearsal.

There are several key pieces necessary for an effective mental rehearsal.

Specific and Detailed

Mental rehearsal must be very specific and highly detailed. You have to practice your performance in your head exactly as you wish to perform it. You do this all the time without being aware of it. When you decide to run errands on Saturday, you imagine yourself doing it first. You see yourself going to the grocery store, dropping off your dry cleaning, and getting the oil changed in your car. You may make a list of these activities, but in your mind you visualize yourself doing them. Then, the next day, you do these activities. You carry out the pictures that you had visualized the day before.

Let's say your goal is to write during your lunch break from work tomorrow. Visualize yourself doing that using as many details as you can. Imagine the numbers of your clock displaying noon, and picture yourself leaving the office and driving to the library, or sitting at the picnic tables behind your building. Imagine how your laptop will feel as you pull it out of your case and set it up. Picture yourself pulling up the file of your work-in-progress and typing away for thirty minutes or however long you plan to write. Imagine the sensations of your fingers on the keys, hear the clicking noise they make as you tap them. Feel your body in the chair, imagine noises, scents, and sights of the place you will work.

Details create the situation you are striving to accomplish *in advance* and help the subconscious mind bring that situation into reality. Mental rehearsal sets up neuron pathways in your brain that simulate the actual event and assist your subconscious mind in making it happen.

Vivid and Emotional

Using vivid mind pictures infused with emotion is another key element for successful mental rehearsal. Remember, emotion is like fuel to the subconscious engine. It creates intention and desire within the conscious mind, which in turn influences the subconscious.

For example, I once watched an Olympic ice skating competition where one of the male competitors was ill with the flu the day before his performance. He became dehydrated and had to spend an entire day in the hospital receiving intravenous fluids.

The next day it was his turn to skate, and even though he was still weak and had had no time to practice, he gave a stunning, practically flawless performance.

In an interview immediately after his performance, a reporter commented that he had looked confused when he finished skating and asked if he were still sick. The skater explained that while he was lying in his hospital bed, he had mentally gone over and over his performance in great detail. He imagined every turn, every spin, and how the ice would feel under his skates. He imagined the roar of the crowd when he finished and how it would feel to take his final bow. He charged his mental rehearsal by experiencing in advance his tremendous sense of accomplishment when the gold medal was hung around his neck. This mental rehearsal was so powerful that when he finished his routine he didn't know if he had actually done it or if it was just another mental rehearsal, and that was why he was confused.

Mental Rehearsal and the Self-Fulfilling Prophecy

Remember the self-fulfilling prophecy concept discussed in the last chapter? When you constantly feed your subconscious mind images of writing success through mental rehearsal, the subconscious mind uses those images to create your reality in accordance with what you're visualizing.

This is why your expectations about writing are so important, because whatever you expect to have happen is what you feed your subconscious by way of mental pictures. Your mental pictures generate emotion according to what you're thinking, and this influences the subconscious in the direction of that emotion. For instance, if you expect to get rejected when you send in a manuscript or query letter, you give that picture and emotion to your subconscious. You think about the rejection letter, what it will look like, and how you are going to feel when it arrives.

You create sensations of disappointment, resentment, anger, and sadness. You may think that you're being "realistic," but actually what you are doing is making that particular situation a reality before it happens.

The Voice of Experience

"I always made sure to be working on a new project. Then when I received a rejection, I thought, 'Yes, but wait until they see this new story. It's so much better, and I know they'll want to buy it.' I stayed open and continued to learn and improve my craft. I'm still doing that."

—Ann Roth

On the other hand, if you feed your subconscious mind pictures of writing success and charge those pictures with elated, happy sensations of fulfillment at having your writing dreams come true, the subconscious mind takes that as a command and eventually makes that your reality. Napoleon Hill called this a Positive Mental Attitude. It's the belief that things will work out in a positive way, no matter what the circumstances.

How to Use Mental Rehearsal in Writing

Mental rehearsal can be used in many ways to help your writing and your writing career. Let's take a look at these methods now and how bestselling authors have used them to find writing success.

Write Scenes

You can use mental rehearsal to both help formulate and write scenes in your stories. Every night, imagine yourself sitting at your desk, writing. Mentally practice each of the steps involved in your writing, from getting to your desk, opening your Word file, and starting to type. Mentally see the scenes that you need to write. This is a technique that author Cheryl Holt uses, although she says it took time and practice to develop the skill. "I do see scenes very clearly, and this is something that comes with practice and experience," she explains. "It was my thirteenth published novel. When I plotted it out and sat down ready to write, I could see every single thing that was going to happen. I have a clear picture of all the scenes in my head, like it's a movie, and then I just watch the movie and put it down on paper."

This type of mental rehearsal of the scenes takes practice, as Holt notes, but all mental rehearsal takes practice. Simply start imagining your scenes before you write. Mentally see yourself writing those scenes. This will program your subconscious to provide the material when you are at your desk.

Practice Your Pitch

Mental rehearsal comes in handy when you are at a conference getting ready to pitch your manuscript or story proposal to an agent or editor. It's a technique that can mean the difference between success and failure, and it's one that many bestselling authors have used.

Here's how you do it. Before a pitch, sit down and relax. Imagine yourself walking into the pitch exuding confidence. You smile and hold your head high. Know what clothes you will be wearing and visualize yourself in this outfit. Rehearse giving a three-line pitch about your writing project with ease. Imagine the response you want the agent or editor to have to your pitch. Hear the dialogue. Imagine questions and how you will respond. Get the pitch down to the most specific details and run through it in your mind as often as possible before your appointment.

Charging the mental rehearsal with positive feelings of success is critical to making it work. Ensure that you infuse your mental rehearsal with an air of confidence and expectation of success. Make sure that you believe in yourself when mentally rehearsing or no one else will believe in you.

Meet Daily Writing Goals

Let's say your goal is to write a novel in a year, and you've set a daily goal of writing one thousand words. Use mental rehearsal to help you meet this goal. Mentally practice getting to your desk, opening your computer, and writing one thousand words. Charge the rehearsal with the good feelings of meeting your short-term writing goal. This rehearsal along with the emotion gives your subconscious mind a command that will motivate and inspire you to write one thousand words the next day.

The Fast-Forward Movie

The *fast-forward movie* is a technique I developed to use mental rehearsal in my own writing life. Basically, it's a step-by-step mental review of how your Vision of Success or your short-term writing goals will be achieved, broken down into "frames." Each frame consists of a single major step on the path to your goal. You create each frame individually, then group them together sequentially like a movie and play it quickly over and over in your head as often as possible throughout the day, and when falling asleep and waking up.

The Voice of Experience

"I have a clear picture of all the scenes in my head, like it's a movie."

—Cheryl Holt

To create your own fast-forward movie, imagine your Vision of Success or your goal and then work backward. Think of five or six major action steps that you will have to take starting now to reach your goal. Each of the major steps will become a "frame" in your movie.

The trick with creating the fast-forward movie is to choose each activity that, in your mind, represents the five or six *most important* steps along the path to completion of your overall goal. These frames will be different for everybody because not everyone has the same challenges to overcome to reach a goal. For instance, it's not a struggle anymore for me to get up early to write, so visualizing myself rising when the alarm rings would not be a frame in my fast-forward movie. But if you are beginning a new writing schedule that you find difficult to maintain, then you would want to include some major action steps toward keeping your schedule as frames in your movie.

Choose the most important steps on the path to your goal and write these down so you can create your own fast forward movie.

Example of a Fast-Forward Movie

Here is an example of a fast-forward movie for a hypothetical writer—we'll call him Ted. Ted is writing a science fiction novel, and his Vision of Success is represented by the image of him winning a Hugo Award. The frames used below are just one set of major action steps that could lead to the achievement of this long-term goal. When you create your own fast-forward movie, choose the action steps that represent the key steps that *you* should take.

1. Frame one shows Ted writing every night after his family is in bed. He creates a mental snapshot of himself in the act of writing at his desk. He adds a lot of details: the house is quiet except for his gentle tapping at the keys, it's dark outside, the dog is curled up under the desk, etc. Ted sees himself writing in the conditions that will actually exist when he writes. Then he adds the emotion: he feels deeply satisfied when he meets his word-count goal, and gets a little burst of euphoria when he checks "writing" off his list for the day.

2. Frame two shows Ted mailing off his completed, polished manuscript to an agent. He has a particular agent in mind, so he visualizes that person's name on the mailing label. He pictures himself at the post office, dropping the envelope into the slot. Ted imagines feeling great about his accomplishment as he watches the manuscript drop into the mail slot.

3. Frame three is an image of Ted receiving a phone call from his ideal agent, telling him how much she liked his book and how

thrilled she is to represent him. An important piece of a frame involving other key people is the actual dialogue that will occur; during your fast-forward movie, you want to rehearse exactly what is going to be said by all parties. So Ted imagines what the agent will say, what he is going to say, and how he will *feel* when this conversation happens.

4. Frame four shows Ted holding his published book. He imagines what the cover looks like, how the book feels in his hands, how heavy is it, what the pages feel like. Adding sensory details makes the imagery more vivid and therefore more powerful. Again Ted adds the emotion of how great it feels to hold his first published book.

5. Frame five shows Ted attending book signings, talking with fans, and again *feeling* great about all of it.

6. Frame six, the last frame, is Ted's Vision of Success. He mentally rehearses standing at the podium accepting his Hugo Award. He sees his name inscribed on the plaque. Flashes go off. He hears the applause. Ted's family beams at him from the audience as he basks in the glow of this wonderful event.

Each of these six frames makes up Ted's fast-forward movie of winning a Hugo Award for a science fiction novel. Ted can rehearse his movie during a period of meditation, when waking up and before going to sleep, while he's driving, while he's standing in line at the grocery store, when he's bored at work, when he's exercising, and so on. He reviews in quick sequence the six frames, over and over again, reveling in the good feelings they create.

It's important to create these frames in advance so you have a ready-made vision of your ultimate goal that you can play in your mind at unexpected times, when you find yourself caught in traffic or waiting in line at the bank. Having a ready-made movie also means you can easily imprint your Vision of Success on your subconscious mind; you don't have to wonder, "Okay, what's my goal and how am I going to get there?" You already know what your goal is and how you're going to get there, and you mentally rehearse taking these steps over and over in your mind until it becomes a reality.

Practice combining the frames into a movie until you get the sequence down pat, then speed it up. As you go through your day, run your fast-forward movie through your mind as often as you can. Every opportunity that presents itself as unoccupied "mind time" should be devoted to running your fast-forward movie.

My Experience with the Fast-Forward Movie

While writing this book, I also wanted to work on a novel. Since I work full-time, I had to use my early-morning writing time for this book, which was under contract. I asked my sub-conscious to give me the solution for how to work on the novel without compromising the quality of my writing time on this book. After two weeks of asking the question, my subconscious provided a picture of me going to the library every day on my lunch hour with my laptop.

So now I had the solution to the writing problem, and the next step was to program my subconscious mind to make it happen. I created a fast-forward movie to do it:

1. Frame one showed me putting my laptop into my car every morning before going to work.
2. Frame two showed me leaving promptly at noon with my laptop and driving to the library. (Remember, you want to pick frames that show major action steps that help you over-come any barriers to the goal. I included this particular frame because my job is demanding and often the things that come up before lunch make it difficult to leave for an hour. This

frame reinforced the notion to my subconscious mind that I would leave at noon to write for one hour.)

3. Frame three showed me sitting in the library, writing. I threw in sensory details like the temperature of the room, the feel of the hard wooden chair against my back, the muted conversation of other patrons.
4. Frame four showed me stacking up the completed pages of my novel.
5. Frame five showed me holding the completed manuscript in my hands and feeling proud of my accomplishment.

I played this movie in my mind every night before I went to bed, every morning when I woke up, and every chance I got while at work, *especially* before lunch because of the barrier noted above. I constantly reinforced the notion to my subconscious mind that at noon I would leave with my laptop for one hour and go write at the library. It had outstanding results. There were a few times when situations arose that prevented me from leaving, but on most days I left at noon and went to the library. This allowed me to meet my short-term goal of writing my second novel while also writing this book.

Mental rehearsal is a proven technique for achieving success in any arena, including writing. Elite athletes have been capitalizing on it for decades and, by following the guidelines laid out in this chapter, you can too. Mental rehearsal is an effective way to program your subconscious mind to help you meet all of your writing goals and boost your creativity. And it's easy to learn and fun to do.

The Writer's Block

Mental rehearsal uses detailed imagery about critical steps necessary to reach a certain goal, and allows you to mentally practice the behaviors that will lead to the attainment of those goals. It is another tool that helps influence your subconscious mind to bring about your desired results. Remember:

- ➠ The mental pictures you create about your writing goals generate emotion, which in turn influences the subconscious mind according to that emotion.

- ➠ The Fast-Forward Movie is a good way to quickly and easily use mental rehearsal throughout the day to reinforce your writing aspirations.

- ➠ Mental Rehearsal can be used to help you meet your daily writing goals, successfully give a pitch to an editor, or accomplish any aspect of your Vision of Success.

CHAPTER FIFTEEN

Creating *Sacred* Writing *Space*

Just as you carve out time in your day for writing, you need to carve out space in your environment to nurture that writing. Selecting a special writing space is a key way to nurture your creativity and honor your muse. Over time, just the act of walking into the area will stir your creative instincts and help you get down to the business of writing.

Styles of sacred writing space are as varied as book topics and the writers who come up with them. Some authors need a secluded room or area of the house to use as their creative workspace. Others take laptops or keyboarding devices to a quiet place, such as a table outside in the garden. Other authors find that writing in a busy, crowded coffee shop has a stimulating effect on their creativity, and some find that people watching can be a great stimulant to creativity.

There are many ways to make any area into a creative space. Decorating your writing area is a way to make it sacred, even if it's just the space around your computer or your laptop case. Even a bustling commuter train can become your creative writing space with a little outside-the-box thinking.

The Creative Space of Famous Writers

While writing *Thinking Places: Where Great Ideas Were Born*, Jack Fleming and Carolyn Fleming extensively researched, visited, and wrote about the creative spaces of famous writers like Ernest Hemingway, Charles Dickens, Jane Austen, Robert Louis Stevenson, Mark Twain, Virginia Woolf, Rudyard Kipling, and many others. They discovered that all of these famous authors had a special place they claimed as their own just for thinking and writing. Sometimes these authors had more than one writing place, and they were not always the conventional offices we think of today. These places were sacred to the authors and no one else was allowed into the space. The rooms were deliberately chosen for their solitude and freedom from distractions. For example, Virginia Woolf wrote in a small building in the rear of her garden. Rudyard Kipling wrote in a large study of the family home in England that no one else was allowed to enter. Ernest Hemingway's most famous writing space is the office at his home in Key West, but even before he was published he always sought out a special writing place. As a young aspiring author, he rented a cheap room that overlooked the rooftops of Paris and wrote longhand in blue notebooks during the early morning hours.

Not all thinking and writing places of famous authors were self-contained rooms, however. Just like writers today, many authors of times past had to make do with unconventional writing places because of large families or a general lack of space. Thomas Carlyle, author of classics like *The French Revolution*, detested noise and was bothered by the slightest sound. Because he grew up in a large family, his writing place was a quiet, secluded ditch near his home. Jane Austen was forced to write, in secret, in a hallway of her family's home. "She had a little chair and a table," says Carolyn Fleming. "She didn't want people to know she was writing so she wrote on small pieces of paper. They had a gate that creaked when someone was coming, so she would quickly change her papers and not let anyone know she was writing."

Any space can be turned into a sacred writing space with a little innovation and determination. William Faulkner is an excellent example of this. As a graveyard-shift worker in a power plant, Faulkner often wrote on a flipped-over wheelbarrow during the wee hours of the night when the town was asleep and the demand for coal at a minimum.

Many famous writers even used walks in nature as a sort of mobile creative space. "The fall of darkness helped Dickens, who walked the city streets of London at night," says Fleming. "Kipling would go out and walk for hours and hours. Wordsworth liked to walk, and the rhythmic pattern of his feet helped his poetry." Walking slowly and methodically like Wordsworth helps the brain get into an alpha state and sets up mental conditions that allow creativity to flow.

Why Sacred Writing Space Is Important

In addition to the famous writers discussed above, all of the professional writers interviewed for this book have a special writing place. To encourage your creativity, it's important that you find some space for writing that is yours and yours alone, too.

When you have a space for writing, it becomes sacred to you over time. It becomes a safe and comfortable place for your muse to emerge. Walking into the space acts as a cue to your subconscious mind that it's time to get creative. Much like a Pavlovian response, simply going into the space and sitting at your desk will energize the creative process.

The Voice of Experience

"If you have this place, just going into it constantly jump-starts the creative process."

—Carolyn Fleming

This sacred writing space also eliminates many of the mundane distractions that eat into your precious writing time. When you have a space that is just yours, you can sit down at your appointed writing time and *write*. You don't have to get the kids' toys out of the way first, you don't have to clear away your spouse's work-related project, you don't have to clean up the dirty dishes that someone else left scattered around the computer. You can simply sit down and get to work.

While you don't want everyone else's belongings in your writing space, filling the space with items that are special and inspirational to *you* is a way to keep you constantly motivated. The items themselves become triggers over time to your subconscious mind and inspire creativity.

Having a special writing space also gives writing and creativity literal space in your life. It's a show of commitment on your part to your writing, and it builds a bridge to your subconscious creativity. Even if you must or prefer to write in a public coffee house, a library, or on a commuter train, there are still things you can do to make that space sacred to your writing.

Create Your Own Sacred Writing Space

The ideal situation is to claim an area in your home that will be yours alone for writing. It could be a spare bedroom, a large closet that is not being used, a storage area off the garage, or a shed or other unused structure on your property. If there is nothing like this available, aim for a secluded and rarely used area of the house, such as a corner in the formal dining room, space in the laundry room, or an area of your bedroom that you can claim as your writing area. You can literally rope off space in a room using ribbon or masking tape on the floor to designate a "no-cross zone" to your family. Folding panels that are used in offices to demarcate cubicles can also be used to designate a corner of a room in your house or apartment as your writing area.

The Voice of Experience

"Once I walk in here and sit down, my body automatically knows, 'Okay it's time to write.' The biggest mistake people make is to ever taint that area. I don't ever come in here to read a magazine. I don't come in here and chat."

—Dianna Love

Your goal should be to create a space that you use for writing and nothing else. Doing this preserves the sacredness of the space. Don't go there to talk on the phone, balance your checkbook, prepare a grocery list, or even to read. This space should be free from distractions, too. Eliminate phones, answering machines, stacks of bills, lists of household to-do items, your kid's schoolbooks, your spouse's work-related projects, and so forth. Devote your writing space to writing and writing-related materials only.

This begs the question of what to do about e-mail and the Internet if you write on a computer that is in this area. The answer is that you either shut down the programs while writing or write on a keyboarding device or a second computer that is not attached to the Internet. Do not allow that intrusion, either physical or mental, into your writing space.

Pump Up the Creativity

After you find your writing space, infuse it with creativity by decorating it with items that you make or select yourself. Whether you use decorations, tokens, books, or knickknacks, your writing space should shout creativity from every corner.

The Voice of Experience

"I decorated the room myself. I painted the walls, sewed the drapes, refinished the antique table I use as a desk, and hung the bookshelves. A lot of creative energy went into the room, and I feel it when I walk in. I've written fourteen books there."

—Robin Wells

Feeling the creative energy of a room is what you are going for, too. Hang drapes in a color that reminds you of creativity. Remember, Chapter 9 discussed how the color green stimulates creativity in most people, so your drapes and other items in your writing space might be various shades of green. Place any items that inspire you to greater heights into your line of vision around your writing table. Hang your collages and other artwork on the walls around you. Place your writing craft books, dictionaries, and thesaurus on shelves within easy reach. Fill the other shelves with books from writers that you admire and seek to emulate. If you write about a particular time in history or about a certain foreign country, place books about these times and places on the shelves, too. Everything around you in this space should ignite your creative state of mind.

Surround Yourself with Success

Your writing space should be a constant reminder of the success you are striving to reach. Anything and everything that keeps you steady on your path to success will aid in releasing your creative mind state and have the added benefit of providing constant impressions to your subconscious mind to make it happen.

"My office screams with symbols and meaning," says novelist Ann Roth, describing the inspirational things she has in her writing space that keep her going. "A poster above my computer proclaims 'Never, never, never give up.' A wire angel hangs over the poster to remind me to follow my heart. There are fairies hanging here and there, to add a bit of magic to the process. There are inspirational sayings tacked here and there. And of course, books. My own books are prominently displayed, and my reference and [writing] craft books are within easy reach."

Many writers choose to put up their list of goals in their creative space to keep the words and motivation flowing. Author Lori Devoti says, "I keep a list of writing- and career-related goals posted on the wall." This is something that I do, too. On a sheet of sky blue poster board, I wrote my overall writing goals and hung it above a collage that has pictures and motivational words of success. Whenever I take a break from the writing or get stuck, I look up and there it is.

Author Jax Cassidy frames her book covers and hangs these on her writing space walls as encouragement to keep writing. "I have all my releases framed on my wall as a motivation," she says. "By seeing my accomplishments, it makes me want to keep writing so I can look forward to another release." Again, this constant immersion in your goals and images of success makes a lasting impression on your subconscious mind, and not only boosts your creative output but leads you down the path to success as you have defined it.

Surround Yourself with Inspiration

Add reminders of success to your creative writing space. Author Fran McNabb visited Hemingway's Key West office and felt so inspired by it that she ordered a picture of the space, which also shows his typewriter. "I hung it where I can see it from my computer," she says. "Knowing that he wrote some of his manuscripts on this simple manual typewriter and not on our sophisticated computers is inspiration in itself. Looking at the picture reminds me of the feeling I had as I stood outside the door to that office on the tour of his Key West home. I held up the tour because I didn't want to leave that spot."

Sometimes writing inspiration comes from sources other than writing, which is okay. Author Brenda Novak surrounds her writing area with items provided by her children. The special tokens provide as much inspiration and motivation to her as writing objects would. "I work in my guest house," she says. "The only plaque nearby is a cross-stitch my daughter made that says, 'A mother listens with her heart.' Almost all the other stuff is from my children, too, most of it things they've made for me. I don't necessarily surround myself with items to keep me focused or draw out my muse—I surround myself with the objects I prize above all else, because looking at them makes me happy."

You can do this, too. Find objects that remind you of times when you felt relaxed, happy, and carefree. I have a photo of a deserted beach at sunset on my desk, which I find helpful to gaze at when I get stuck or frustrated with the writing. Your items might be from your children, too, or your spouse, or a dear friend. Whatever makes you smile and generates enthusiasm to keep going should be in your sacred writing space.

Create Sacred Space Anywhere

Some authors like Allison Brennan prefer to write in noisy coffee shops. Brennan sequesters herself from the distraction by listening to certain choices of music, as discussed in Chapter 10. Other authors like to switch writing locations from time to time when they get stuck or need a little extra boost to get going for the day; for instance, they might switch from writing at their desk to writing on a laptop outside in the sunshine. I will often go to the public library with my laptop to write on days when the creativity doesn't feel "on" at my writing space at home. Many authors who hold down traditional jobs frequently write on their commute in a noisy train or car.

If writing in a nontraditional setting like this is your preference, or if you have to do this because your living situation does not permit you to carve out sacred space right now, there are things you can do to create an atmosphere of sacred space even in the midst of a crowd. Here's how:

Use Special Materials

To create an atmosphere of sacred creativity in a public location, acquire supplies that you will use only for writing during your selected time. In other words, don't just dig a pen that you write with every day at work out of your purse or briefcase. Buy pens that you use *only* for writing. Most people have a preference in pens, so buy a box of your favorites and keep them to the side as your special writing pens.

Do the same thing with what you write on. Designate a pad of paper that will be for your writing purposes alone, not one that has grocery lists, your kid's soccer practice schedule, and work contact numbers scrawled in the margins. Keep this pad just for your writing.

The Voice of Experience

"I have only a few requirements before I start writing. First, I absolutely must have breakfast and a strong cup of coffee. Also, I try to get my exercise in before I get to work. And finally, I want a supply of unlined typing paper and just the right sort of gel pen."

—Tess Gerritsen

Next, get a few small items that are motivational to you and place them somewhere that you can see them while you write. It can be something as simple as a motivational quote that you tape to the top of the pad of paper. If you use a keyboarding device or laptop, set the small item or tape your motivational quote to the edge of the screen before you start writing. When you're finished writing, put all these items away, together, in a certain place, and only bring them out at your next writing session.

Create a Portable Office

A good way to create sacred writing space on the go is to create a portable office. You can take this office with you anywhere: to cafes, to restaurants, to the library, on the train, to the park, to your kids' gymnastics lessons, and on airplanes. Creating a portable office is simply another way of triggering your subconscious mind to get creative, no matter where you are.

Get a briefcase, backpack, large purse, or laptop case and put all of your writing materials together in that case. Decorate the case in ways that inspire you and that designate it as your portable sacred writing space. You can use magic markers to draw on the case, paste or tape motivational pictures or sayings to the case, or write your goals on the case. If you feel self-conscious about putting these things where others can see, do it on the inside, where you will see it when you open the case. The key is that *only* your writing things will go in this case—nothing else. That's what makes it sacred.

The Voice of Experience

"I wrote one whole book at a specific Starbucks, and I started the next book and couldn't write there, so I found a different Starbucks."

—Allison Brennan

I have a canvas bag that holds all of my writing supplies: my favorite pens, yellow notepads, and folders filled with research for the project I am working on at the time. The key item is a bright pink, flexible binder that has numerous sections that I can move around at will. The tabs are made from a special type of plastic that allow me to erase the ink so I can change the headings on my sections easily whenever I want to. (You can buy such a notebook at any office supply store.)

In some sections I include my goals for the writing project I am currently working on, along with a check sheet indicating where I am in the project. Because I have a daily and weekly word count goal, I keep a running tally of where I am in both so, if the weekend comes and I am short on my weekly word goal, I can make it up by Monday.

Another section I call "projected dates." Here, I file a worksheet that contains my expected dates of completion for each chapter of the book. This allows me to stay on track with my progress. For instance, I list each week and beside that I write down where I should be in my total word count each day. I project out for every week it will take to get the book written, building in adequate time for revisions on the initial drafts. Other sections include notes for the book and an outline if I made one.

I put this pink binder as well as my laptop and other special writing materials in my canvas bag. When I arrive at the library at noon every day, as soon as I pull out that pink notebook my subconscious mind is triggered into a creative state.

A portable writing office is a good idea even if you have a steady place to work, because sometimes it helps to change locations to get the creativity flowing again. This is a successful tactic used by many professional writers.

"I have a great office at home," says novelist Candace Havens. "It's lined with bookshelves and has my favorite art on the walls. I've been writing at the same desk for eight years, and when I sit down, I'm ready to get to it. That said, sometimes I want a new location. I grab the laptop and sit on the couch with my dogs all around me. It's funny how moving to another room can help get things going."

Sometimes taking a laptop out to the patio of your home or the public library generates more creativity than a carefully designed space in the home. That's the experience of author Susan Elizabeth Phillips. She has a beautiful home office. The space contains a custom-built desk, a bay window that looks out to the backyard, designer cabinetry, files that were designed especially for her, glass doors on the cabinets so that she can look at her books, and a shelf where she has put pictures of readers and other tokens and souvenirs. But she can't write in that room. "I can revise there," she explains. "But when I have to write I take my laptop into the living room, or out to the porch. I have to get away from the business around it."

As you can see, creating sacred writing space is one of the keys to unlocking your creative potential and freeing your creative mind. But there is a lot of flexibility about what you can use for your writing space. The key idea is that your space is used for writing and because of that, it becomes sacred over time. That has a positive impact on your writing and your ability to quickly access your creativity. If you do not have a creative writing space, make plans for one now, even if it's the portable office described above. Anything is better than nothing, and the effects on your writing will be immediate.

The Writer's Block

Sacred space to write is as critical to your success as a writer as time to write. This space eventually becomes associated with writing and helps jump-start the creative process whenever you enter it. Remember:

- ◆ Your writing space should be for writing alone; eliminate your kid's homework, your spouse's work projects, stacks of household bills, and any other nonwriting intrusions.

- ◆ To reinforce the creative process, do not do anything but write in your sacred space.

- ◆ If you cannot designate a space in your home to write, create a portable space by putting together a notebook for your current project and use it only for your work-in-progress.

CHAPTER SIXTEEN

Writing *Routines*
for Maximum
Creativity

G etting into a creative state of mind is as simple as one-two-three when you use a routine. Studies have found that you can actually train your brain to get into an intensely focused and creative state just by doing the same activities in the same way each time you begin a task. It's a way of signaling the mind to move from an outwardly focused beta state to an inwardly focused alpha state. Writing routines that produce a state of mind conducive to creativity can be simple or more involved, depending on your level of need and interest. Even short routines can aid your creativity level by helping you make the transition from ordinary life to your daily writing session.

Focus

In *Time to Write*, I presented two writing schedules that require a quickly focused attention state—the "mini-blocks-of-time" writer and the "any-opportunity" writer. The mini-blocks-of-time schedule calls for writing in short intervals, usually five to twenty minutes. These brief periods of writing time are shoehorned into your day in advance. For example, you know that at two-thirty every afternoon, you have twenty minutes of undisturbed time that you can write while your preschooler naps, so you set a timer after you put her down and write nonstop during that period. The any-opportunity writer keeps a notebook or laptop at the ready all the time and seizes unexpected free minutes in which to write; perhaps while stuck in traffic on the interstate, while waiting in line at the bank, or in between meetings at work. For both of these writing schedules, since the writing time is very brief and sometimes sporadic, it is especially important that you focus and not allow your mind to wander. Those brief periods of writing time must be capitalized on to the fullest extent, and it will be hard for you to focus if one part of your brain is making a shopping list while another part is trying to plot out the next chapter in your novel.

Focus is also required for longer periods of writing time. Since many aspiring and established writers have to squeeze writing in around jobs and family obligations, getting the most writing out of any chosen schedule is critical to success. Setting up a pre-writing routine alerts your right brain that it's time to get creative and helps you maximize your writing opportunities.

As we discussed in Chapter 14, studies of the brain have demonstrated that a mental review improves performance in any area because it helps you to *focus*. Routines are a form of mental preparation because they shift you from an outward focus of paying the water bill to an inner state of concentration, relaxation, and creativity. Routines alert your subconscious mind that you are about to write. They help your conscious mind focus and become receptive to your subconscious creativity by saying, "Pay attention. We're about to get creative now."

The use of a pre-writing routine is a common practice among many successful writers, and it can be as simple as what Ernest Hemingway did before writing. Hemingway was believed to always have sharpened a dozen pencils before he looked at his work-in-progress. Even a simple routine like this can assist you in getting into a creative mind state quickly and easily.

The Voice of Experience

"If you don't focus you'll never finish the book. And you'll never be a published author if you have nothing to sell."

—Novelist Fran McNabb

Writing routines are especially important these days because life has become so hectic for most people. You cannot sit down and write your three daily pages when you are still harried from a hard shift at work. Establishing some type of routine before you write will help you move from "world-mode" to "creative-mode" and allow you to capitalize creatively on even brief periods of writing.

Create Your Pre-Writing Routine

There are many ways that you can incorporate a routine into your writing schedule to take advantage of a routine's benefit.

Get the Mundane Out of the Way

Your pre-writing routine can be as simple as getting mundane tasks out of the way before you begin writing. Simply create a list of activities that you need to do before you start. This is like mental housekeeping. First do all the little tasks that nag at you while you're trying to write, and then you don't have to worry with them while you are in a creative state of mind. The purpose of a routine like this is to eliminate any possible distractions that can crop up during the actual writing session. This is something that novelist Fran McNabb does; she reads and answers e-mail straight away to avoid having to open nonwriting computer programs throughout the day. "The first thing I do is get e-mail out of way," she says. "I cannot stand going into the computer during the day while I'm supposed to be working."

You can create a similar routine by doing the following before sitting down to write:

- Making your coffee or tea
- Checking your e-mail and then closing out the program
- Gathering your research materials around you or printing them off the Internet and then closing out the browser
- Gathering your writing supplies, and taking care of any loose ends that may distract you once you begin to write
- Putting the clean dishes away
- Folding the laundry
- Making business calls
- Taking care of any other task of daily living that distracts you from your writing

Putting a time limit of thirty minutes (or less) on completing these tasks will help you get them out of the way quickly and not eat into your principal writing time.

Get Your Writing Space Ready

Preparing their writing area for the day's work is another routine used by successful authors. That's how novelist Kerrelyn Sparks does it. "I write longhand for the first draft, so I get things ready around my favorite comfy chair," she says. "A glass of ice water on the table, a spiral notebook and pen, an afghan to keep my feet warm, a clock so I won't completely lose track of time and forget to pick up the kids from school. I pull up the blinds on the window by my chair, so I can look at the green plants and grass outside. I get comfy in my recliner, and then I let go."

To use this routine, make a list of what you need around you to write. Perhaps you need a pillow for your back, a glass of ice water, red pens for editing, and so forth. For me, I also like to have a dictionary and a thesaurus nearby. Many writers keep a shelf of writing craft books near their desks. Gather all these materials and put them within easy reach before you begin writing. That way, you won't have to get up and search for something during your actual writing session, and the process of collecting your items will get you into a creative state of mind.

The Voice of Experience

"To focus one side of the mind elsewhere frees up the creative side."

—Bonnie Edwards

Meditate or Use Progressive Relaxation

As you have learned, relaxation and creativity go hand in hand. Setting aside a few minutes to run through your progressive relaxation routine prior to writing is a good way to settle your mind, capture a state of focused attention, and open a pathway to your subconscious. Ten or fifteen minutes is usually adequate for this type of routine. Many successful writers like Lori Bryant-Woolridge, author of *Weapons of Mass Seduction* and other novels, mediate before they begin writing, which helps still the mind. "I sit down and get quiet for twenty minutes," she says. "It's little things like that that get my mind disciplined and focused."

Read Inspirational Material

An excellent routine for getting into a creative state of mind before writing is to read inspirational material about goal setting, achievement, or the psychology of success from authors such as Brian Tracy, Napoleon Hill, Zig Ziglar, or Wayne Dyer. These achievement-focused books often generate lots of enthusiasm for moving ahead with your goals and provide major doses of motivation to work toward success.

You can also read works by other authors that you admire and seek to emulate. Set aside fifteen minutes to read one or two chapters from a novel that inspires you to write.

Light Candles

Lighting candles around your writing area is an elegant way to cue your subconscious mind that it's time to start writing, and it can add a certain mystical quality to your writing space. A candle engages all of your senses; you see the warm flame, you feel the heat on your face, you smell the fragrance, you hear the hiss and sputtering of the fire as the wax melts. Peppermint, cinnamon, and eucalyptus are crisp scents that stimulate your brain.

Gazing into the flame can also help you get centered, still your mind's chatter, and allow you to focus on the work at hand. I once took a writing workshop that required each of us to light a white candle at the beginning of each writing session and extinguish it after we had read our work aloud. It was only a one-day event, but after three writing periods I discovered that lighting the candle had an immediate effect on me. I slipped into writing mode simply upon striking the match, and watching the flame for a few seconds helped me connect to my writing voice quickly.

The Voice of Experience

"Many days I'll burn a candle, usually peppermint. It's a fresh scent and makes me happy, and clears the cobwebs on my brain."

—Candace Havens

Write Randomly

Sometimes the worst distractions to a creative mind state come from inside your own head. An effective way to quiet the chatter in your brain and get into a mental state of focus is to set an egg timer for ten or fifteen minutes and then write without editing on a blank pad of paper. Author Susan Elizabeth Phillips frequently uses this routine when she has trouble focusing on her work-in-progress. "It's a very useful creative tool for me, sitting down with the yellow pad and my favorite pen and writing randomly. It helps to focus my monkey chatter brain," she explains. "Every time I get stuck plotting I get to the quiet time with the yellow pad. I use a kitchen timer, set it for fifteen minutes, and that time I have to stay in my seat. Once you get through that first ten minutes or so things start coming more easily."

You set the egg timer because you want to put a time limit on this routine. Give yourself fifteen minutes to write randomly, and then turn your focus to your principal writing for the day.

Get Rid of the Negative

If you find yourself facing writer's block, create a routine that helps you get that block out of the way. For example, author Jacquelyn Mitchard has a special routine when she finds herself facing a problem in her writing. "If I'm in a fix, I use a few grains of red Hawaiian salts given me by a friend, dissolved in a bowl, and try to 'dissolve' my problem in that red pool, which I then empty out in nature," she says.

I have a similar routine that I use when I'm stuck in my writing. I visualize my writing problem flowing out of my head and into a simple glass of clean water. I then pour the water down the drain while I imagine the writing problem disappearing along with the liquid. You can also write the problem on a sheet of paper and then shred it, tear it up, or flush it down the toilet. Routines like this are simple to do and they work because they symbolically allow you to dissolve, empty, or discard the writing problem and easily eliminate any blocks.

Reread the Previous Day's Work

Part of your pre-writing routine can be to review what you previously wrote in order to regain focus on the work at hand and stimulate the creative process. Some writers call this "getting back into the story." Rereading the previous day's work primes your creative pump and gets you back into the groove of your story. It can also generate enthusiasm for the project because it gives you a jumping-off point for that day; you are not just sitting down cold, trying to think of where to begin. Most importantly, your subconscious mind has been working on your story while you were away from your desk, and rereading the previous day's work allows any solutions or new ideas generated by your subconscious to flow into your conscious mind.

Routines often serve multiple purposes, and novelist Jax Cassidy points out that another benefit to this rereading routine is keeping the entire project on track. "I like to read my blurbs or the last chapter I've worked on before I begin," she says. "The repetitive reading helps me to remember where I'm going and keeps me on track."

If you choose to make rereading the previous day's work part of your pre-writing routine, again put a time limit on it. Any routine should not be allowed to eat into your primary writing time.

Use Special Items to Represent Your Muse

Some writers use a small object as a representation of their muse in order to tap into their creative mind when they sit down to write. This object can be anything that is personal to you and represents writing and writing success. For instance, Charles Dickens had a little green monkey on his desk to represent the muse. Rudyard Kipling kept a small canoe nearby for good luck.

Contemporary writers use small special items to represent the muse, too. Author Yasmine Galenorn has a little porcelain cat on her desk. "I have had her since I was seven years old," she says. "She's become my writing mascot." Author Judi McCoy surrounds herself with angels given to her by fans. "I count on those angels to keep me working," she says.

Other writers use items that are inspiring and motivate them to keep going. Novelist Berta Platas keeps a certain cup on her desk given to her by a friend who was already an established writer. "She went to a Romance Writers of America convention and came back with a cobalt blue cup that said 'RWA: 1.8 billion in sales,'" Platas explains. "I used that exclusively to drink out of while I was writing my first book that sold, because I was going to be a piece of that 1.8 billion. And it worked. It certainly came true."

The Voice of Experience

"I have a painted rock in my purse that I reach in and rub any time I'm feeling down. It says 'Dream it.' To me, if I can dream it, imagine it, visualize it, I can make it happen."

—Faye Hughes, author of *Afterglow* and other novels

For your writing muse, select meaningful items that represent what you want writing to bring to your life. Novelist Ann Roth keeps items that will help bring good fortune as well as good writing. "On my computer desk sits a see-through briefcase filled with gold-foil chocolates, signifying riches," she says, "also a gold foil–covered chocolate Rita [award], meaning excellent writing." Roth also keeps nearby a little stuffed ladybug for luck, as well as a small Hotei, the Buddhist god of good fortune and happiness.

Choose any item that is meaningful to you and that represents the muse or provides inspiration and motivation to write. A couple of years ago, I went to a workshop where I was given a small smooth gray rock to represent the muse. I set the rock on a special place near my computer and whenever I get stuck, I look at it and ask the "muse" for help.

An established writing routine is a good tool for focusing the mind and gaining access to your subconscious creativity. Writing routines can be as simple as making a cup of your favorite tea to more complex ones like meditating for a few minutes before you start writing. If you wish, you can emulate Ernest Hemingway by sharpening a dozen pencils before you start working on your manuscript, or you can gather up items at conferences, or from your children, or light scented candles to begin your next writing session. Using routines consistently is key to engaging your creative mind. Putting a writing routine into place is an excellent way to jump-start your creativity.

The Writer's Block

By helping you to focus, a writing routine gets you into a creative state of mind quickly. You can train your brain to get focused and in a creative state by practicing a consistent routine. These writing routines will help you shift from day to day life to your creative writing session. Remember:

- ➼ A writing routine can be as simple as lighting a scented candle or reading a few pages from a book by an author who inspires you.

- ➼ Many writers reread their previous day's work to jump-start the creative process.

- ➼ A good writing routine that helps get rid of negative thoughts about your abilities is to write these thoughts down on paper, then tear the paper up and flush it down the toilet.

CHAPTER SEVENTEEN

Collaging
and Other
Art Forms

W riters are creative people, and one of the characteristics that creative people share is a broad range of interests. You can use this to your advantage by employing other forms of art to program your subconscious mind to help you complete writing projects and meet your writing goals. The techniques in this chapter are designed to help you do that by capitalizing on the subconscious-influencing formula of genuine intent + repetition + burning desire.

Using other forms of art to aid writing is an easy leap for most writers because of their natural affinity for creativity in many forms, not just the written word. When your writing is blocked or you need a break, engaging in another art form is a great way to keep that contact with the subconscious mind open while giving your conscious, disciplined self a rest.

How Art Inspires Writing

Working in other art forms besides writing can be fun. It gives you a chance to expand your creative repertoire and get in touch with your inner child again. Children are naturally good at creating in whatever outlet is presented to them. They will finger-paint, draw, color, build things with Legos, make items out of play-dough, and experiment in many ways with no judgment and no focus on the outcome. They are 100 percent process oriented. It doesn't matter to a child if the dog they made out of clay looks like a cow. The focus for a child is the fun they had in doing it.

This is the state you want to return to as well. As adults, we often become results oriented. We edit, criticize and judge our work as we go along. We sometimes erase, wipe off, tear down, and undo our creations before we even get started with them. Being in this critical state of mind is not conducive to creativity, but returning to a childlike wonder of watching the creative process unfold before you can be a great aid to your writing.

The Voice of Experience

"When I am stuck in a scene and can't seem to get the words to flow, I like to do art projects like painting with acrylics or working on my artist trading cards."

—Jax Cassidy

The key to using other art forms to inspire your writing is to keep your mind open. When you use them, don't edit or judge yourself as you go along. Let that childlike portion of yourself come out and have fun.

Make a Writing Collage

A good way to jump-start the creative process when beginning a new writing project is to collage about it. Collaging stimulates intention and desire to finish the writing project, and hanging the finished product on the wall and looking at it every day provides the repetition piece of the formula. Collaging is an affordable art project that requires no special skills or training. Many successful writers use this technique as a means to bring characters into sharp focus and develop their creative ideas. It's an easy way to get the creative flow moving when beginning a new project or when you experience writer's block. Collaging can stimulate ideas, reveal new directions in the story, and generate motivation and enthusiasm for a project.

Before you begin, decide what you want to collage about; you might choose your novel's characters, the setting, or the timeline. Perhaps you want to generate enthusiasm for a new or stalled project, or you're looking to manifest a particular goal. (We'll go over each of these options in more detail in just a minute.) Jot down notes about key points you want to cover, or make a sketch on notebook paper of themes and what you want the collage to look like. Don't overanalyze it though. Sometimes it's fun to have a general idea of what you want to collage about and then flip through magazines, cutting out whatever phrases, words, or photos appeal to you in that moment. Looking at pictures and phrases in magazines boosts your creativity, and you will feel inspired about your project and motivated to complete it.

Below are some items you can use when making your collage. This is by no means an exhaustive or prescriptive list. Use whatever materials feel right for your project:

- Poster board in a color that appeals to you
- Magazines for pictures related to your project
- Magic markers in various colors
- Glitter in various colors
- Gel pens in various colors
- Ribbon and yarn in various colors
- Feathers
- Stamps and stickers
- Glue (stick glue works best)
- Scissors

Once you've gathered your supplies, flip through the magazines and cut out any pictures, words, or phrases that are consistent with the theme of your collage. Lay the poster on the floor and arrange your items. When you're satisfied with it, glue everything down. How you arrange the items on the board and how you space them is entirely up to you. Let the items overlap if you wish, or leave space to write inspirational words or phrases next to the pictures. Last, give the collage a title.

The Voice of Experience

"I go through magazines and pull out pictures and things like that if I can't quite get a visual on a character."

—Dianna Love

Hang the dried collage near your computer and gaze at it for a few minutes before you start writing, whenever you look up from your writing, when you're done with your writing, and any other time you can. Let the images soak into your mind. These images and phrases combined represent your writing goals and your writing career. They will motivate you, inspire you, and act as powerful action commands to your subconscious mind.

Now let's look at the various ways you can use collaging as a way to help your writing and program your subconscious mind.

Collage Your Characters or Plot

You can make collages that include photos that display significant physical traits of your characters, demonstrate occupations or actions that your characters will take, reveal details of the city or location in which your story is set, or that identify key points in your plot or nonfiction work.

The Voice of Experience

"I make collages of character faces like a ready reference. I don't want to read that they have green eyes, so I just look up and describe what I'm looking at."

—Berta Platas

Collaging your story provides a constant picture to your subconscious mind of all the pieces of your project. It provides, in a single glance, the totality of your book to your subconscious mind. It makes the story, the setting, and the plot real. It is a concrete, physical representation of the idea and can serve as a ready-reference while writing. Looking at your story collage before writing will reorient you to your writing and help you access that creative zone again.

Bestselling author Dianna Love used collaging in the early stages of writing her novels. Love is also a visual artist and has painted billboards and other works of art throughout her career. She now uses collaging in her writing to connect with characters and help clarify them in her mind. She strives to create a certain attitude with her collage rather than a specific representation of her characters. "I go through magazines and pull out pictures and things like that if I can't quite get a visual on a character," she says. "I'm not looking for the physical attributes so much as an expression or a look in their eyes."

Select magazines that contain the types of advertisements that fit the demographics of your characters or the types of actions they are likely to engage in. For example, if your story is about a young couple who are adopting a baby, cut pictures from periodicals that target young men and women. If you are collaging about plot points for a thriller novel, look for magazines that have lots of pictures of fast cars, James Bond-type men in fashionable suits, or pictures of people engaged in exciting activities like bungee jumping, sky diving, and so forth. Choose photographs, phrases, or words that represent the key points of the plot that you want to illustrate.

The Voice of Experience

"I will use pictures of certain people. Jerrod Butler is a good one. It helps me if I have someone in mind."

—Monica McCarty

Collage Your Story's Setting

If your story has certain key landmarks that you want to describe vividly in your novel, choose pictures that are similar to these and use them in your collage. Some writers make a collage that is representative of the setting of their story, like a map. Travel magazines and brochures are a good source of photos of exotic places that make interesting novel settings, and the statistics that most travel brochures carry are helpful for bringing realism to your book. Using a collage of your story's setting makes it real in your mind and also helps you keep facts straight as you're writing. For example, you might collage the town square and your characters' homes in relation to it, the kids' school, or a particular body of water that your character has to drive across in key scenes.

Collage to Get Motivated

Collaging generates enthusiasm because it inspires you to write about that topic. I once accepted a freelance magazine assignment but afterward discovered that I had little enthusiasm for the topic. It was difficult to write the article because I wasn't really that interested in the subject matter. However, I had taken the assignment and was obligated to complete it, so I collaged about it to generate some enthusiasm. I found words and pictures in magazines that put a positive spin on the topic and that programmed my subconscious to generate motivation to complete the assignment. For example, I combined words to make phrases like "I am always inspired" and "Writing is fun" and put them on the poster board. Whenever I went to the computer to work on that article, I would gaze at the collage for a few minutes and let the images and words soak in. The process worked. The collage always created a positive feeling inside me regarding writing and toward that project in particular, and I was able to finish the assignment and turn the article in on deadline.

Collage Your Writing Goals

Collaging about your writing goals is a good way to motivate you to work toward them. Gather images and words that represent action steps that you need to take toward your goals. If one of your goals is to become a freelance journalist within twelve months, clip pictures of anything that represents freelance journalism to you. You could choose pictures of typewriters, a person in the act of writing, covers of the magazines you want to write for, and so forth. Collage about the baby steps you need to take to meet your goals. If your goal is to write one page per day, clip the words "one page per day" and paste them everywhere on your collage, using images of typewriters, pens, paper, and other symbols of completed writing. Or use images of people sitting at tables or desks, writing, or a combination of the two. The possibilities are endless. What's important is that you use words and pictures that are meaningful and inspirational to you and your writing process.

The Voice of Experience

"If I happen to be thumbing through a magazine and spot a model or something else that triggers an emotional reaction or an idea, I'll definitely clip it."

—Brenda Novak

Collage to Overcome Writer's Block

The wonderful thing about collaging is that you can use it for so many things related to writing. You can even use it to overcome writer's block. Because writer's block is really just a noncreative state of mind, the trick is to give messages to your subconscious mind that get you back into a creative state of mind. Collaging is a great way to do this because images and pictures are a powerful tool to use when communicating with your subconscious.

I once made a collage to help me overcome a period of writer's block. Because the image of flowing water represents for me the act of words flowing from my mind, down my arms, and into my fingers, I found lots of pictures of water flowing: out of a shower head, over a cliff, down mountains, through forests, into bathtubs, and so forth. I cut the pictures out, glued them to the poster board, and wrote "words flow" in purple ink beside them all. I hung the poster beside my computer and every time I got stuck in the writing, I gazed up at this poster board and let the images of water flowing seep into my brain. After a few minutes, my subconscious provided me with more words to put onto the paper.

Other Ways to Use Collaging

There are dozens of ways that you can use collaging to help build a bridge to your subconscious mind and unlock your creativity. Here are just a few:

- When writing nonfiction, collage the key points of your article and the ideas you want to get across in the story.
- When writing your family's memoirs, make copies of old photos and use the prints to form a collage that will inspire memories. This also creates a sense of nostalgia that will translate to the page.
- Make a collage of your writing timeline, with photos to represent each stage of the project. This will also help you stay on track with your goals and ensure you finish the piece by your deadline.

Success Collaging

"Success collaging" is a form of collaging that you use to manifest your writing dreams, or your Vision of Success. It's different from collaging your individual writing goals. With your individual goals, you are working on specific tasks that will move you toward completion of your writing projects, but collaging about your success is broader in scope. You are collaging about what writing success means to you, and that will look different for everyone because it's based on your unique Vision of Success.

To begin, first think of your Vision of Success. What does your ideal writing life look like to you? Do you have a special office for writing, perhaps a desk that overlooks the ocean or a garden? Will income from books or magazine articles allow you to reduce your hours at your job so that you can spend more time with your family? What types of books and articles are you writing?

Similar to creating your fast-forward movie, define the major steps along the path to your Vision of Success and the major outcomes that you want writing to bring you. Then flip through magazines and cut out pictures that represent each of these outcomes. Or simply cut out photos that represent your end goal and what you want your life to look like when you reach your goal of becoming a successful writer. Paste your pictures on a piece of colorful poster board and hang it on the wall next to your computer. Remember to give it a title to help focus the message to your subconscious mind.

Here is an example of success collaging from my own writing life. As I've mentioned, I used to live in a busy subdivision in Atlanta that backed up to a major thoroughfare to the interstate. The noise from the constant traffic interfered with my ability to write. I made a goal of relocating to a quieter place in which to live and work, and decided to collage about it. I purchased two pieces of bright yellow poster board and six home decorating magazines and went to work. I clipped out pictures that represented the ideal home and workspace for me. I used one piece of poster board for the exterior of the house and office and the other for the interior. Among other things, I chose a picture of a home office that overlooked a garden and another picture that showed a house with a body of water in the backyard. I used different-colored Sharpies to name the pictures and enhance the specific details I was sending to my subconscious mind. For example, next to the picture of the office, I wrote, "My office overlooks a garden." Next to the lake in the picture, I wrote, "My house backs up to a body of water."

I titled the collage "My Magic Cottage." I hung the poster boards up on the walls of my office where I would see them every single day. When I came in to the office or took breaks from my work, I would look at the collage and imagine how it would *feel* when I was actually working and writing in such a lovely space.

Three years after making those collages, an unexpected opportunity allowed me to move to a quieter location. Today, I am writing this book in a small house that very much resembles a cottage; it sits on land adjacent to a bay, and my office window overlooks a lush garden. Every aspect of the collage came true.

Other Ways to Use Art for Writing

Collaging is one way to use the visual arts to help your writing creativity, but there are more ways to do this, too. All of these techniques are fun and allow you to capitalize on your innate creative talent while programming your subconscious mind to help you reach your writing goals.

Write Your Name on Bestseller Lists

The trick to using other art forms to help you with your writing is to do things that send a strong message to your subconscious mind. Say your goal is to make the *New York Times* bestseller list. A good way to get this command entrenched firmly into your subconscious mind is to put it there via a continual visual means.

Clip out the printed bestsellers lists from the newspapers and write your book title and name in the number one slot, then tape the revised list by your computer. Stare at it whenever you look up from your writing. This sends a clear, declarative picture to your subconscious mind about what you want to have happen.

The Voice of Experience

"I've got print-outs of the *New York Times* list, *USA Today*, and *Publisher's Weekly* on my office wall with my books taped into the number one slot!"

—Bella Andre

In his book *Be My Guest*, entrepreneur Conrad Hilton talks about how he used a similar technique to manifest his dream of beginning a famous chain of luxury hotels. Financially destitute as a young man, Hilton never lost faith in his dream. He had a Vision of Success. One day in 1931, he stumbled across a picture of the new Waldorf hotel—one of the swankiest hotels at the time—in a magazine. Hilton clipped out the picture and wrote "The Greatest of Them All" across the photo. Hilton's intention was to buy the Waldorf hotel and turn it into one of his own. He held on to this photo until he had enough money to buy a desk, at which time he placed the photo under the glass desktop. In so doing, he gave his subconscious mind a constant reminder of what he was striving for. He burned the image of the plush Waldorf onto the screen of his mind, and fueled it with emotion of how it would *feel* when he finally owned that hotel. Fifteen years later, "The Greatest of Them All" became a Hilton hotel.

Draw Your Book Covers

The perfect way to manifest a goal in the form of a published book is to draw, color, or paint your future covers. You do not have to be artistically inclined to do this. Simply get a piece of colored poster board and either cut it down to book-size proportions or create an oversized image of your cover. Using watercolors, acrylics, magic markers, and gel pens, draw what you want your future book cover to look like. If you can find magazine pictures that resemble your characters, include those on the cover. Write your title at the top along with your byline. Hang the cover by your computer where you will see it every time you sit down to write. You can also make a mock book cover by using computer graphics and a color printer.

Drawing your future book covers in vivid detail sends a strong message to the subconscious. While I was writing my novel *Grave Secret*, I drew what the future cover was going to look like as a way to motivate myself to keep getting up at 3:30 A.M. to write before work. I drew the two main characters on the cover in a particular position, and a house on fire behind them. About six months after the book was under contract, the publisher e-mailed me a file of the cover art. It was precisely as I had drawn it, down to the smallest detail.

Using other art forms to communicate with your subconscious mind is a great way to inform your writing. It's also a fun way to stay in a creative mind state even when you are not actively writing.

The Writer's Block

Writers are creative people, and many creative people enjoy a wide variety of interests, including working in other art forms. Using other forms of art to aid writing can help you get unblocked or recharge your creativity when you need a break from your work-in-progress. Remember:

- Writing collages are fun and easy to make using glue, scissors, poster board, and pictures clipped from magazines.

- Make collages that help you attain your daily writing goals or your Vision of Success, or that help you flesh out a particular project.

Your Creative Mind Toolbox

As a writer, your subconscious mind is your most powerful tool. Learning to access its treasure trove of riches and program it to help you reach all of your writing aspirations is the key to all writing success. This book has given you the tools to do both. Let's review all of the techniques that you now have at your command to become a successful writer.

❑ You have a working understanding of your mind's components and how each of these components operate. You know how to recognize your anti-writer and have easy tools for combating it in your daily writing life.

❑ You know the benefits of creating. As a creative person, you understand that you share certain characteristics with other creative people and that creativity enriches your life. You understand that creating in the form of writing gives you a sense of accomplishment, adds meaning and value to your life, and satisfies your Burning Desire to Write.

❑ Relaxation is now a tool in your arsenal that you can employ whenever you need it to access your subconscious mind.

❑ Your dreams are an important means of subconscious communication, and you know how to increase your chances of remembering your dreams and how to use them for creative material. The hypnagogic state is highly useful for writers, and you have the means to use that naturally occurring state to your creative benefit.

❑ You know how to communicate with your subconscious mind using subconscious image projection in the form of mirror gazing, and by using ideomotor responses with a pendulum.

- You know how to use music and nature to your creative benefit.
- Positive programming statements, positive suggestions, and mental rehearsal are all a part of your daily life as a writer. You know how to capitalize on the power of your subconscious mind to create your reality as a writer and meet all of your writing aspirations.
- You have created a sacred writing space and a writing routine. You understand the benefit and importance of both of these tools for maximizing your creativity. Special items that represent the muse surround you in your writing space, be it in your home or a portable office in your briefcase.
- Last, you know ways to use other forms of art to inspire your writing and engage your creative mind. Using other art forms is a technique that you can now use to meet your writing aspirations.

You are now in possession of all the tools you need to free your creative mind and become a successful writer, tools that bestselling authors use every day to accomplish their short- and long-term writing goals. By using the techniques presented here, you can follow in their footsteps and make all of your writing dreams come true.

It's been a pleasure bringing these tools and techniques to you, and I hope you will let me know how they work for you. Please email me after you try them at *Kelly@KellyLStone.com*. I would love to hear from you.

Good luck, and happy writing!

Bibliography

Austen-Leigh, James Edwards. *A Memoir of Jane Austen by Her Nephew.* (New York, NY: Oxford University Press, 2008).

Edwards, Frank. *Stranger Than Science.* (New York, NY: Citadel Press, 1959).

Fleming, Carolyn, and Jack Fleming. *Thinking Places: Where Great Ideas Were Born.* (Victoria, BC, Canada, Trafford Publishing, 2007).

Hill, Napoleon. *Think and Grow Rich.* (Hollywood, CA: Wilshire Book Company, 1999).

Hilton, Conrad. *Be My Guest.* (New York, NY: Prentice Hall, 1957).

McCullers, Carson, and Carlos L. Dews. *Illumination and Night Glare: The Unfinished Autobiography of Carson McCullers.* (Madison, WI: University of Wisconsin Press, 2002).

McTaggart, Lynne. *The Intention Experiment.* (New York, NY: Free Press, 2007).

"Migrant Mother, 1936," EyeWitness to History, *www.eyewitnesstohistory .com* (2005).

Moody, Dr. Raymond, with Paul Perry. *Reunions: Visionary Encounters with Departed Loved Ones.* (New York, NY: Ivy Press, 1993).

Shelley, Mary Wollstonecraft. *Frankenstein, Third Edition.* (London: Henry Colburn and Richard Bentley, 1831).

Stevenson, Robert Louis. *Across the Plains.* (London: Chatto & Windus, 1892).

Stillwell, Arthur Edward. *Live and Grow Young.* (New York, NY: Youth Publishing Company, 1921).

Tracy, Brian. *Goals! How to Get Everything You Want Faster Than You Ever Thought Possible.* (San Francisco, CA: Berrett-Koehler Publishers, Inc., 2004).

Ueland, Brenda. *If You Want to Write.* (Saint Paul, MN: Graywolf Press, 1987).

Wallace, Robert K. *Jane Austen and Mozart: Classical Equilibrium in Fiction and Music.* (Athens, GA: The University of Georgia Press, 1983).

Index

Ackley-McPhail, Danielle, 109, 116

Action plan, 20-21

Andre, Bella, 59-60, 82, 200

Anti-writer, 14-21
  action plan, 20
  counteracting, 16-21
  countering statements, 17-19
  notebook, 17
  and preconscious mind, 14-15
  resistance to writing, 16
  sabotage, 16
  setting yourself up for failure, 16
  and subconscious mind communication, 88-89

Archer, Zoe, 102, 108-9, 132

Art, 189-201
  best seller lists, writing name on, 199-201
  collage, 191-99
  drawing book covers, 201
  inspiring writing, 190-91

Austen, Jane, 76, 92, 110, 164, 165

Belief, 141-48
  and suggestion working together, 142-43
  and support, 145-46

Beverly, Jo, 4, 105, 114

Brain waves, 35-37

alpha, 35, 63

beta, 36

delta, 35

and relaxation, 36-37

theta, 36, 63

Brennan, Allison, 60, 72, 105, 107, 144, 171, 173

Bryant-Woolridge, Lori, 182

Burning Desire to Write, 26, 30, 130

Candles, 182-83

Carlyle, Thomas, 165

Cassidy, Jax, 97, 115, 170, 190

Character interaction, 113-20
  benefits of, 114-15
  coffee with your characters, 119-20
  dialogue, 115-16
  interviewing characters, 116-18
  open-ended questions, 117-18
  paraphrasing, 118-20

Collage, 191-99
  for characters or plot, 193-94
  items for, 192
  for motivation, 195
  other uses, 197
  for setting, 195
  success collaging, 198-99
  for writer's block, 196
  for writing goals, 196

Color, 92-93
Conditioned response, 102-3
Creative visualization, 136-38
    bedtime visualization, 138
    bouquet of flowers, 137-38
    and short term goals, 136-37
    Vision of Success, 136
    of words flowing, 137
Creativity, 23-31
    benefits of, 25-27
    and brain waves, 35-37
    characteristics of creative
        people, 27-31
    defined, 23-25
    and music, 101-11
    and nature, 91-99
    and sacred writing space,
        168-69

Devoti, Lori, 15, 169
Dickens, Charles, 114, 164, 165,
    185-86
Doubt, 15
Dreams, 47-60
    attitude of expectation, 49
    editing help, 54-55
    and famous writers, 58-60
    journal, 50-51
    rapid-eye movement
        (REM) cycles, 55
    recording middle of the
        night material, 55-56
    soliciting guidance and feed-
        back from, 56-58
    solutions, 51
    steeping yourself in writing,
        52-53
    and subconscious, 47-48
    subconscious access to,
        48-49

Edison, Thomas, 64
Edwards, Bonnie, 52, 69, 181
Einstein, Albert, 92
Eureka moment, 28

Fast forward movie, 157-61
    author's experience with,
        160-61
    example, 158-60
Faulkner, William, 165
Fleming, Carolyn, 164, 165, 166
Fleming, Jack, 164
Focus, 178-79
Ford, Henry, 29
Fouault, Jean, 83
Freethy, Barbara, 63, 145-46
Freud, Sigmund, 5

Galenorn, Yasmine, 11, 24, 26,
    106, 186
Garden, 96-97
Gerritsen, Tess, 29, 56, 172

Hart, Raven, 59
Havens, Candace, 114, 174, 183
Hemingway, Ernest, 164, 170,
    187
Hendrix, Lisa, 66, 108
Hill, Napoleon, 59, 126, 154
Hilton, Conrad, 200-1
Holt, Cheryl, 37, 155, 157
Howe, Julia Ward, 64-66
Hughes, Faye, 186
Hypnagogic state, 62-69
    holding an arm up, 68
    marbles over bowls, 67-68
    and pajamas, 68-69
    using, 66-69
    and writers, 64-66

Index cards, 17-19
Inspirational reading material, 182
"I" sentences, 147-48

Kipling, Rudyard, 164, 186
Kopil, Su, 119

LaFevers, Stephen, 49
Lange, Dorothea, 28
Left brain/right brain, 34-25
Love, Dianna, 64, 167, 192, 194

Maxwell, Cathy, 25, 86, 106, 107, 137
McCarty, Monica, 185, 194
McCoy, Judi, 54, 93-94, 138
McCullers, Carson, 92
McNabb, Fran, 56, 170, 179, 180
Meditation, 181-82
Mental rehearsal, 150-61
    and daily writing goals, 156
    fast forward movie, 157-61
    and pitches, 155-56
    and scene writing, 156
    and self-fulfilling prophecy, 153-54
    specific and detailed, 151-52
    vivid and emotional, 152-53
    in writing, 154-58
Mind, 4-12
    vs. brain, 4
    conscious, 6-7
    preconscious, 7-8
    subconscious, 3, 8-10
Mirror gazing, 76-79. See also Subconscious mind projection
Mitchard, Jacquelyn, 51-52, 104, 134, 184

Moody, Raymond, Dr., 68, 76
Mullins, Debra, 59
Muse, 185-87
Music, 101-11
    Baroque, 109
    and conditioned response, 102-3
    as a creative tool, 102-7
    lyrics that inspire, 107
    mood music, 108-10
    play lists, 103-4
    for relaxation, 109-10
    and scenes, 105-6
    and themes, 106-7
Musical instrument, 110-11

Nature, 91-99
    color, 92-93
    decorating your writing space, 99
    finding, 95-96
    garden, 96-97
    inspiring creativity, 93-94
    plants on desk, 97-98
    to relieve tension, 94-95
    silence of, 98
Negatives, ridding, 184
Notebook, 17
Novak, Brenda, 156, 170, 196

O'Keefe, Molly, 24, 98, 107, 115, 136, 142

Painter, Kristen, 30, 50, 110
Pajamas, 68-69
Pavlov, Ivan, 102-3
Pendulum method of subconscious communication, 82-88
    setting up a code, 84-85
    using the pendulum, 85-88

Phillips, Susan Elizabeth, 75,
145, 175, 183
Plants, 96-97
Platas, Berta, 53, 104, 186, 193
Positive Declarations and Imagery (PDI), 130-33
consistency, 133
self-fulfilling prophecy,
131-33
Positive Mental Attitude, 154
Pre-sleep state, 62-69
Programming statements,
134-35
Progressive relaxation, 37-42,
181-82
program, 39-40
short, 41
uses of, 42

Random writing, 183-84
Relaxation, 33-42
and maximum creativity, 34
and music, 109-10
progressive, 37-39
progressive relaxation program, 39-40
short progressive relaxation,
41
Re-reading previous work,
184-85
Resistance to writing, 16
Roth, Ann, 118, 154, 169,
186-87
Routines, 177-87
candles, 182-83
focus, 178-79
mediation, 181-82
mundane tasks, 180
muse, 185-87
negatives, ridding, 184

pre-writing, 179-87
progressive relaxation,
181-82
random writing, 183-84
reading inspirational material, 182
readying your writing
space, 181
re-reading previous work,
184-85

Sabotage, 16
listing sabotaging actions,
19-20
Sacred writing space, 163-75
creating anywhere, 171-75
creating your own, 167-71
creativity infusion, 168-69
and famous writers, 164-65
importance of, 165-66
and inspiration, 170-71
materials for, 171-72
portable office, 173-75
readying as part of routine,
181
and reminders of success,
169-70
Scott, Walter, Sir, 72
Self-fulfilling prophecy, 131-33
and mental rehearsal,
153-54
Setting yourself up for failure,
16
Shelley, Mary, 64
Sleep. See Dreams
Sparks, Kerrelyn, 34, 65, 93, 96,
110, 181
Stevenson, Robert Louis, 58-59,
76, 164
Stone, Robert M., 84

Subconscious communication,
  81-89
    pendulum method, 82-88
Subconscious mind, 3, 8-10
    accessing, 10-12
    and anti-writer, 88-89
    and doubt, 15
    gold mine, 125-39
    images, 71-79
    and suggestion, 141
Subconscious mind projection,
  71-79
    and authors, 76
    techniques, 73-76
    and writing, 73
Subconscious programming,
  126-30
    burning desire, 130
    creative visualization,
      136-38
    example of, 139
    intention, 127-29
    programming statements,
      134-35
    repetition, 129-30
    Positive Declarations and
      Imagery (PDI), 130-33
Suggestion, 141-48
    action, 143
    and belief working together,
      142-43
    commitment to writing,
      144-45
    "I" sentences, 147-48
    recording suggestions,
      146-47
    and support, 145-46
Support, 145-46

Tesla, Nikola, 24

Tracy, Brian, 147
Twain, Mark, 164

Ueland, Brenda, 69

Vision of Success, 129-30, 136
    and fast forward movie,
      157-60
Visualization. *See* Creative
  visualization

Wells, Robin, 57, 94, 111, 168
White, Sasha, 66
Woolf, Virginia, 92, 164
Wordsworth, William, 165
Writing space, decorating, 99.
  See also Sacred writing space

About the Author

Kelly L. Stone (author) started a successful writing career while holding down a full-time job. Her articles and essays have appeared in *Family Circle, Writer's Digest, Cat Fancy, Chicken Soup for the Soul,* and *Cup of Comfort.* Her novel, *Grave Secret* (Cincinnati, OH: Mundania Press, 2007) was called "powerful" and "well-written" by Romantic Times Book Reviews. Her first book for writers, *Time to Write: More Than 100 Professional Writers Reveal How to Fit Writing Into Your Busy Life* (Avon, MA: Adams Media, 2008) features advice from 104 successful authors, including more than forty national bestselling authors, and demonstrates how to find time to write no matter how busy you are. *Time to Write* was nominated for the American Society of Journalists and Authors Outstanding Book of 2008 Award. Kelly is a licensed mental health counselor and holds a Master's degree in counseling from Florida State University. She can be reached via *www.KellyLStone.com.*

Robert M. Stone (compact disc author and performer) received his Bachelor of Arts degree with Honors in psychology from the University of Florida and his Master of Science degree in counseling from Auburn University. He has worked with hypnosis and subconscious communication since 1976 and has conducted thousands of hypnosis sessions helping people resolve problems. He lectures on hypnosis and subconscious communication to professional and civic groups and has appeared on television and radio programs discussing the power of the mind and how to use it. He can be reached at *rstone@geohanover.com.*